First World War
and Army of Occupation
War Diary
France, Belgium and Germany

48 DIVISION
Divisional Troops
474 South Midland Field Company Royal Engineers
1 May 1915 - 28 October 1917

WO95/2751/1

The Naval & Military Press Ltd
www.nmarchive.com
Published in association with The National Archives

Published by

The Naval & Military Press Ltd

Unit 10 Ridgewood Industrial Park,

Uckfield, East Sussex,

TN22 5QE England

Tel: +44 (0) 1825 749494

www.naval-military-press.com

www.nmarchive.com

This diary has been reprinted in facsimile from the original. Any imperfections are inevitably reproduced and the quality may fall short of modern type and cartographic standards.

© Crown Copyright
Images reproduced by permission of The National Archives, London, England, 2015.

Contents

Document type	Place/Title	Date From	Date To
Heading	WO95/2751/1		
Heading	48th Division BEF 1st Sth Mid'd Fld Coy RE. Became 474th S.M. Fld Coy RE May 1915 Oct 1917		
Heading	48th Division 1/1 S.M. Field Coy R.E Vol V 1-31.5.15		
War Diary		01/05/1915	31/05/1915
Heading	48th Division 1/1st S.M Field Coy R.E Vol VI 1-30.6.15		
War Diary		01/06/1915	30/06/1915
Heading	48th Division 1/1 S.M Field Coy R.E Vol VII		
War Diary		01/07/1915	31/07/1915
Heading	48th Division 1/1 S.M Field Coy R.E Vol VIII From 1-31.8.15		
War Diary	Hebuterne	01/08/1915	31/08/1915
Heading	1/1 S.M Fd Coy R.E Feb Vol XIV		
Heading	48th Division 1/1st S.M. Field Coy R.E Vol IX Sept 15		
War Diary		01/09/1915	30/09/1915
Heading	48th Division 1st S.M. Field Coy R.E Vol X Oct 15		
War Diary		01/10/1915	31/10/1915
Heading	48th Division 1/1 S.M Fd. Co. R.E Nov 1915 Vol XI		
War Diary		01/11/1915	30/11/1915
Heading	48th Div 1/1 S.M. Fd. Co. R.E Dec Vol XII		
War Diary		01/12/1915	31/12/1915
Heading	1/1 S.M. Fd Coy R.E. Jan Vol XIII		
War Diary		01/01/1916	11/02/1916
Heading	1/1 S.M Fd Coy R.E Vol XV		
War Diary		12/02/1916	29/02/1916
Heading	1/1 S.M Fd Coy R.E Vol 16		
War Diary		01/03/1916	31/07/1916
Heading	48th Divisional Engineers 1/1st South Midland Field Company R.E. August 1916		
War Diary		01/08/1916	31/08/1916
Heading	48th Divisional Engineers 1/1st S.M. Field Coy Royal Engineers September 1916		
Heading	War Diary Of 1/1st S.M. Field Coy R.E 48th Divn From 1st Sept 1916 To 30th Sept 1916 Vol 21		
War Diary		01/09/1916	30/09/1916
Heading	War Diary Of 1/1st South Midland Field Co R.E 48th Division From 1st October 1916 To 31st October 1916		
War Diary		01/10/1916	31/10/1916
Heading	War Diary Of 1/1st South Midland Field Company R.E. 48th Division From 1st November 1916 To 30th November 1916 Vol 23		
War Diary		01/11/1916	30/11/1916
Heading	War Diary Of 1/1st (S.M.) Field Company R.E. From 1st December 1916 To 31st December 1916 Vol 24		
War Diary		01/12/1916	31/12/1916
Heading	War Diary Of 1/1st (South Midland) Field Company R.E. From 1st January 1917 To 31st January 1917		
War Diary		01/01/1917	31/01/1917

Heading	War Diary Of 474th (S.M) Field Company R.E. From 1st February 1917 To 28th February 1917		
War Diary		01/02/1917	28/02/1917
Heading	War Diary Of 474th (South Midland) Field Coy. R.E.		
War Diary		01/03/1917	31/03/1917
Heading	War Diary Of 474th (S.M) Field Coy R.E. From 1st April 1917 To 30th April 1917		
War Diary		01/04/1917	30/04/1917
Heading	War Diary Of 474th (South Midland) Field Company R.E. From 1st May 1917 To 31st May 1917 Vol 29		
War Diary	Epehy	01/05/1917	31/05/1917
Heading	War Diary Of 474th (S. Mid) Field Coy R.E For Month Of June 1917 Volume 30		
War Diary		01/06/1917	30/06/1917
Heading	War Diary (A.F.C. 2118) Of 474th (S. Mid) Field Coy R.E. for Month of July 1917 Volume No.31		
War Diary		01/07/1917	31/07/1917
Heading	War Diary (A.F.C. 2118) Of 474th (S. Midland) Field Company R.E. (T.F) for Month of August 1917 Volume 32		
War Diary		01/08/1917	31/08/1917
Miscellaneous	Casualties August 1917		
Heading	War Diary Of 474th (S. Mid) Field Coy R.E (T.F) September 1917 Volume 33		
War Diary	Peselhoek	01/09/1917	30/09/1917
Heading	War Diary Of 474th (S. Mid) Field Coy R.E For Month Of October 1917 Volume 34		
War Diary		01/10/1917	31/10/1917
War Diary	W. Canal Bank N. Of Ypres	01/10/1917	04/10/1917
War Diary	Siege Camp (A.20.d.91)	10/10/1917	14/10/1917
War Diary	ACQ	15/10/1917	16/10/1917
War Diary	Bertonval Farm	17/10/1917	28/10/1917

woqs|275|11

48TH DIVISION

BEF

1ST STH MID'D FLD COY RE.
BECAME:-
474TH S.M. FLD COY RE.

MAY 1915 - ~~MAR 1919~~ Oct 1917

To ITALY

121/5513

47 GSM
27th Division.

1/1 S.M. Field Coy. RE

Vol II 1 — 31.5.15

Nov '15

474

Army Form C. 2118.

WAR DIARY
or
INTELLIGENCE SUMMARY
(Erase heading not required.)

Hour, Date, Place	Summary of Events and Information	Remarks and references to Appendices
May 1	The Company marched from ERQUINGHEM to DOUDOU FARM arriving abt 7.20 p.m. (owing to orders received at 11.30 a.m. not being received till 3 p.m.)	Move to DOU DOU FARM. Attached to S.M. Div.
2	Church parade attended by 3 Company at PONT DE NIEPPE	
3	Bomb making begun, cleaning billets. Equine transferred from ERQUINGHEM to ARMENTIERES. Bomb making continued — Engine set up & sand	
4	One section working on 2nd line — new trenches & wire for flamenco belts — also cleaning firestore — work finishing up at DOUDOU FARM	
5	Work begun on subsidiary line in PLOEGSTEERT WOOD* Bomb a. before a. 5th (* Infantry. 3 reliefs of 150 men)	
6	do	
7	do	
8	do — 4.0.00 bond completed	
9	do — Majority of C.o.s attended Divine Service in the afternoon	
10	as 8th — Night work begun by 2 S.E.s on Hills 63 (2 reliefs of 200) (Rapunty)	
11	Same section on Hill 63 N, one section on works in wood	
12	do. (2 reliefs on hill 63) — Equine broken down	
13	do. (one relief of 200 men only) +	
14	do. — work in PLOEGSTEERT wood completed. Only one relief of 200 men on Hill 63	

Army Form C. 2118.

WAR DIARY
or
INTELLIGENCE SUMMARY

(Erase heading not required.)

Instructions regarding War Diaries and Intelligence Summaries are contained in F. S. Regs., Part II. and the Staff Manual respectively. Title pages will be prepared in manuscript.

Hour, Date, Place	Summary of Events and Information	Remarks and references to Appendices
May 15	Work begun on carrying road from FARM west of PIGGERIES to N.W. corner of wood. ORES Sapper, 3 reliefs of 100 infantry. Two sections on Hill 63. One section at Sand. Pontoon bridge begun. Remainder of company has batts at PONT de NIEPPE.	La Cpl Lewis + 2 Sappers returned from hospital.
16	Work as on 15th — Sanitation	
17	Do.	
18	Do.	
19	Do.	
20	Night work. No 1 Sec has rest for the day — 1500 pontoon bridge finished. No 2 Sec only on night work. No 2 Sec had rest for the day — 400 bozen of pontoon bridge during PONT de NIEPPE.	
21	The Company attended baths at PONT de NIEPPE — Acting 2nd Cpl Spicer returned to Lee Cpl for dislodging of arm.	2nd Lieut J.V. Thomas returned to Company
22	A barrel of gunpowder exploded during the filling process at 8 a.m. Gunsappers Lee Cpl R Hands, Sapper FTJ Holley, CE Winder, WL Stokes + a civilian named Le Fevert were killed and sappers H Titley, WJ Wright, EA Jones, G Drinkwater, FR Knowles + Cpl DJ Gardner were seriously injured. Sapper Cpl Fear, GA Newby, W Furby + P.J Allam + Sergt. RH Smith being slightly injured	# NCOs + 3 Sappers killed. 2 NCOs + 9 Sappers injured. Capt Hazegood went to BOULOGNE sick.
23	Work as on 23rd — Installation of baths capable of providing hot baths per hour complete at DOU DOU FARM. At night work begun on support trench in rear of trench 39	
24		

WAR DIARY or INTELLIGENCE SUMMARY

Army Form C. 2118.

Hour, Date, Place	Summary of Events and Information	Remarks and references to Appendices
May 25	Work in previous diary - part of the company attended a lecture at PONT DE NIEPPE	
May 26	Work as on 25th - Burial of Sapper Tilley reported	Sapper Tilley died
27	Do on 26th	
28	Do	
29	Do — Sapper E.A. Jones died in result of explosion on 23rd. Sapper A. Evans wounded on night work	Sapper Jones died. Sapper Evans wounded
30	Do — 1500 sandbags issued. Sappers Godfrey and Radford wounded on night work	Capt Hodgson returned to duty
31	Work the night - 150 inf: 11pm Dawn on Support Trench, 150 dawn to 6am on hill 63 near Chateau LA HUTTE, 50 y 3.30 to 6.30 am at the Chateau, 200 .8.30 to 12 & 200 12 to 2.30 on hill 63 making salient on forward slope in front of Villa ROZENBURG. Work as on 30th but no party of 200 available. Nuodeitin a night work	

31/5/15

J.C. Gibson
Major
1/1 Field Company
South Midland R.E.

48th Division

1/1st S.M. Field Coy RE.

Part VI 1 — 30.6.15

Army Form C. 2118.

WAR DIARY
or
INTELLIGENCE SUMMARY
(Erase heading not required.)

Hour, Date, Place	Summary of Events and Information	Remarks and references to Appendices
June 1 – 6 *	The Company continued work by night & early morning on 2nd line defences. One section working in trench road. Poster boxes erased to make on Ht 42. Communication trench from S 39 to Mud Lane begun	
7		
8	Coy in Stadt Reserv — Voluntary Service (C.E.)	
9	Twelve arrivals for huts on Hill 63 –	
10	2nd Lt. J.S. Watling joined 2/I.R.P.2 Coy	
11	Baths, Inspection by G.O.C. No. 1 Sec. practices fastening Company in extension & filling Brigadier & then Battalion & areas on H. line.	
12	Sunday – Voluntary Service (C.E.)	
13	Company took over left sector of line, but work handed	
14	over to 2/1 th worked on 1/1's rd with one civilian gang	
15 – 18th	70th Coy (K's army) attached for instruction	
19th	Coy went out Bde Reserve	
* 2 w/d	Redoubts on top of 63 begun	

Army Form C. 2118.

WAR DIARY
or
INTELLIGENCE SUMMARY

(Erase heading not required.)

Instructions regarding War Diaries and Intelligence Summaries are contained in F. S. Regs., Part II. and the Staff Manual respectively. Title pages will be prepared in manuscript.

Hour, Date, Place	Summary of Events and Information	Remarks and references to Appendices
June 20 – 23	The company was attached to Brigade to Reserve. The work was *Reprise* party trenches – General's trip – "from Meppe to Chateau Rosenburg – Cavalry road – huts. Putting in the 20 & 21 Coy hauled into & from mines. On the 22nd 2nd/Field Eng Richard lost to bear. The Brigade (with Coy attached) moved to trenches nr hillet near Metteren and 11 miles by night. Stan & hands on to 7th Coy	2nd/Field Richard went on leave
24		
25	marches to Vieux Berquin by night – 4 miles	
26	marches by night to GONNEHEM – 15 miles	
27	hauled at 5 pm to ALLOUAGNE. Bivouacked	2nd/Field Richard returned
28	moved into billets. blown wins & village. Previous service	
29	Still – Service. Upper Athens	
30	&c.	

J. Cherrill
Major
O.C. 1st. Field Co.
Midland R. E.

121/6344

1/1 S.M. Field Co, R.E.

WAR DIARY

or

INTELLIGENCE SUMMARY

(Erase heading not required.)

Army Form C. 2118.

Hour, Date, Place	Summary of Events and Information	Remarks and references to Appendices
July 1. — 3	Company in Bri'd Reserve near ALLOUAGNE. Work from 5 a.m. Drill, extended order, Bayonet fighting, Advanced guards, Rear attack on Trenches, Reconnaissance.	
" 4 — 5	Do. — + Pontoon Practice a.m.	Capt Hodges went on leave
6	Do. — Pontooning at CH.PHILOMEL	
7 ; 8	Do.	
9	Do. The Coy took part in Bde Attack practice at Night	
10	Pontooning + drill in the afternoon	
11	The Coy moved at 8 a.m. to bivouac in the BOIS des DAMES at point 36B Square 28 b 15.	2nd Lt Penman went on leave
12	The Coy cut pickets in wood — piece spud it for trench mor. frame. 30 am moved at 1 pm above ground. In the afternoon the Coy moved to MAZINGARBE arriving Pontoon + Trestle Stays at NOEUX les MINES	
13	11 pm. Pontoons + Trestles moved to LABOURSE. At 1.30 am the Coy moved returns to BOIS des DAMES. Supper at 3.30 pm the Coy returns to Pontoon at 8.30 pm arrive at 6 pm. Picket cutting resumed.	
14, 15 16	Orders from above — improvement of trench for motors.	Capt Hodges returned
17	Coy moved at 6.30 a.m. to BELLERY	

WAR DIARY or INTELLIGENCE SUMMARY

Army Form C. 2118.

Hour, Date, Place	Summary of Events and Information	Remarks and references to Appendices
July 18, 19	Company moved at 11.45 to BERGUETTE Station, arrived 2.30 pm. Entrainment complete by 4.30. Train left 5.20 – arrived at DOULENS at 10.30. Detrainment complete by 12.15 – marched to SARTON	
20	Coy Rests at SARTON	
21	Proton Lt sent to AUTHIE. Coy marched at 11.20 pm to COIGNEUX & bivouacked in field	
22, 23	Remained at COIGNEUX, still – Reconnaissance by officers.	
24	Advance party to HEBUTERNE – No 2 Sec & transport to SAILLY en ARTS – remainder in evening to HEBUTERNE. Horses remained at SAILLY	
25	Cleaning billets – work on redoubt – 9 Sothern Officer – trade left work parties. Repair of two retained pumps began.	
26	Work on redoubt continued – Old trenches & 39 team repairing entrances.	
27	As 26 – Stores coming in from SAILLY	
28	But am first works hours 6–9 pm, 3–7 am – Work on cable & pumps at Roman returns	
29	NE 7 am 6 pm. Both pumps running	
30	No further parties available 3–7 am – night work in wiring 6 sappers	
31	Working parties as on 30 t. but hours 8.30 am – 12.30 pm and 1.30 pm to 5.30 pm	

H. Olwood
Major
1/1 S.M. F.G. R.E.

121/6607

48th Division

1/1 S.M. Field Coy R.E.
Vol VIII
From 1 - 31. 5. 15

WAR DIARY or INTELLIGENCE SUMMARY

Army Form C. 2118.

Hour, Date, Place	Summary of Events and Information	Remarks and references to Appendices
August 1–31 HEBUTERNE	The Company remained at HEBUTERNE attached to 145th Bde. One section at a time returned to SAILLY taking charge of R.E. Store there and working on 2nd line. On the 1st Sergt. Harris was wounded - its first on working party in town Ypres. Work carried out during Period includes:- Wiring of entire defences up to north of S.E. face. Completion of Scheme of trenches on S.E. & S.W. faces. (Parts very difficult, being hit as trenches have traverses. Parallels of tops, dug outs for Local Reserve - now complete. Sewer Hetaut mule watering parties were kept on the go for 16 hours daily. Communications of new Comm. Trench DEMONVALLIERS, deepening of said trenches from it. Bricking of BIRON and REMAUD left nearly completed: parties contents of Imp. R.E. Dy. not of Dy. not for B.D. HQ: beginning of water laying from front to trenches delayed by non-arrival of Stores tentatively (flanges). Pumps were run - with slight check - all the month. Town Drainage - to turface hole - was arranged. Four or five have worked in low locality.	

WAR DIARY or INTELLIGENCE SUMMARY

(Erase heading not required.)

Army Form C. 2118.

Hour, Date, Place	Summary of Events and Information	Remarks and references to Appendices
Aug 1-31 HEBUTERNE	One Officer went on leave 2nd Lt. Tapp Aug 19-26. Carpenters smiths were busy throughout on dugout frames, Splint trails for Them, & on trench boards, Stump covers and shelters in fear Rifle rest, pump repairs reconstruction and general work. A riveleurs concrete M.G. emplacement was started in the KEEP. Strand light remained at AUTHIE under Johnson & Poulsom. 2/1 P.G.Coy. On the 31st a new section of Brigade to Brigade to Brigade & other trenches, also new dug out in PASTEUR was proceeded with. Working parties throughout the month were frequently made owing to Depletion of Battalions & paid to the System of relief which caused frequent cancellation of the normal parties. Not much night work was required.	2 Lt Tapp on leave

WAR DIARY
or
INTELLIGENCE SUMMARY

(Erase heading not required.)

Army Form C. 2118.

Hour, Date, Place	Summary of Events and Information	Remarks and references to Appendices
Aug 1–31 HEBUTERNE	On the 30th two Officers & 153rd P.O.C. & n.c.o's for 154th F.C. on arrival for & nucleus attachment  RClement Major Comp 1/1 S.M. F.d Co, RE 48 Div	

48

1/1 S M Fd. Coy R.E.
Feb
Vol XIV

121/6950

48th Division

1/1st S.M. Field Coy R.E.
Vol IX
Sept. 15

Army Form C. 2118.

WAR DIARY
or
INTELLIGENCE SUMMARY

(Erase heading not required.)

Hour, Date, Place	Summary of Events and Information	Remarks and references to Appendices
September 1st – 7th	Work continues in HEBUTERNE SECTOR – Section 4 Officers & 153 O.R. 154th Coy RE attached for instruction till 5th.	Major J.T. Cheevers with a team
8th		Lt Horstead with a team
9th		Major Cheevers returns
10th 11th 13th	Coy moved to ROSSIGNOL Fe (B Sec having gone into reserve on 11.5th) all horses & vehicles being collected there. One section sent to cut timber etc in WARNIMONT WOOD. D Company was employed on the Corps line one section bring sand daily truck to the Bde. Corps line working parties were provided by B Sec in Reserve. 300 in morning & 300 in afternoon. Small parties & work of about 200 also provided by B Sec in reserve	Lt Horstead returns 18th (Bnt Fontaine)
20th 21st	Two Officers & 1 section returns to HEBUTERNE Company moved to HEBUTERNE, one section to SAILLY, horses remaining chiefly at ROSSIGNOL Fe	
22nd 24th	Work fully resumed at HEBUTERNE – parties as before Found dumps (sand) near front line in anticipation of attack. Afternoon working parties carried storm.	
25, 26	R.D.Fy out. Carrying of sapper complete except for carrying to dumps. Took a no of infants who pushed & built Cruise half done Working parties 100 morning & afternoon. At night work finished off in second	
27, 28		
29 30		

Briefing of SOMS & REVEL continues also work on road. Night work a —

PASTEUR

J.T. Cheevers
Major

121/7368

48th Division

1st S.M. Field Coy. R.E.

Vol I

Oct 15

WAR DIARY or INTELLIGENCE SUMMARY

(Erase heading not required.)

Army Form C. 2118.

Hour, Date, Place	Summary of Events and Information	Remarks and references to Appendices
October 1st	Section at SAILLY and no 2 Sn moved to ROSSIGNOL	
2nd	Remaining section moved to ROSSIGNOL. Work on Carp line, & in BOIS du FAY. Details on Pumps at COUIN. Road mending & drill.	
3rd	+ training at COUIN; well sinking at CATERREUX; Carpentering & drill.	
4th – 7th	Programme as on 3rd.	
8th	14 wagon parties on COUIN Road & 34 infantry. Saw &	
9th	Engine removed from BOIS du WARENIMONT set up at ROSSIGNOL.	
10th	Visited by new C.E.	
11th	Football match v Bridle Batt: & afternoon – Carp bath hutes	
12th – 13th	Work in COUIN Road continues + – BOIS DU FAY, as well as Carp line, Pumps & Champs 1st	
14th – 15th	No parties for Carp line – Brigade Change Carp Change + HÉBUTERNE; no 2 Sn at SAILLY	
16th – 19th	Communication trench (Inland) to Warwick Brigade. Any work on PASTEUR continued. Work on Fort BRIGGS MICHELSON, ABLAIN KEEP by night also June in PASTEUR	

Army Form C. 2118.

WAR DIARY
or
INTELLIGENCE SUMMARY
(Erase heading not required.)

Hour, Date, Place	Summary of Events and Information	Remarks and references to Appendices
Sept 19th	Night work on Trench 31 January & still fire	
20th	Brigade change - No San particular	
21st–27th	work continued. Pas a day 31 September Pipes	
	line carried on at VERCINGETORIX.	Lt Richard back on leave 27th
28th	Brigade Change	
29th	with continued - wiring on BG6L & high	
30. h. 31st	Company moved to AZZATTZZAZZ ROSSIGNOL	

[Stamp: 1st S. MIDLAND FIELD CO. R.E. T.F.]

H. Cheswell
Major
1/1st S.M.F. Co R.E.

48th Division

121/7637

1/ S.M. B. Co. R.E.

21.9.15

IX 3

WAR DIARY or INTELLIGENCE SUMMARY

(Erase heading not required.)

Army Form C. 2118.

Hour, Date, Place	Summary of Events and Information	Remarks and references to Appendices
November 1 — 13	Company at ROSSIGNOL WOOD. Two sections on Corps line with 4 parties of 12 infantry from 9—4 daily; one section in Bois Outre with 3 parties of 75 infantry. This work moved on Nov to Bois de BUS. The last day work on 10000 five foot hurdles. One section found details for (a) work about the billet (b) water supply and steam for Baths at COUIN (c) installation of 2nd water system at these baths finished Nov (d) completion of supply for water carts and horse troughs at COIGNEUX finished Nov (e) water supply at new COUIN site.	2nd/Lt. / V. Thomas on leave Nov 3rd — 13th
14	No. 4 Sn moved to SAILLY, No. 1 Sn to HÉBUTERNE.	
15 — 19	Remainder of Coy moved to HÉBUTERNE leaving behind at ROSSIGNOL all drivers and 6 carpenters and sawmen. Work at HÉBUTERNE as usual. BdE supplied 3 parties of 100 men daily 8 am — 12 noon, 1.30 pm — 5 pm and 4.30 pm to 8.30 pm. Day work includes work on GENEVIÈVE	

WAR DIARY
or
INTELLIGENCE SUMMARY

(Erase heading not required.)

Army Form C. 2118.

Hour, Date, Place	Summary of Events and Information	Remarks and references to Appendices
Nov		
20th	Several Shelters, FORT BRIGGS, Roads, Water Scheme &c night work wiring in Battle Reserve Line, revetting at FORT BRIGGS & JEAN BART. Arrangements was made with troops in 6 sector to supply parties of 8 men a night in Post CLIFFORD under Sapper supervision. Brigade Clamp	16th. Sapper Leonard Damaged by Saw.
21–24	Work as before - many dug-outs had traverses rounded squarely as before - many dug-outs had traverses rounded squarely & in "trinity corner".	22nd 2nd Lieut E.M Browne joins the Company.
25	Returned our work and m'trinity corner). Supply of 8 for picket reported for JEAN BART trench was difficult to obtain. On night of 25/16 Lt. Strickland and 3 Sappers accompanied the left party of the morning by the 6th Glo's for an "exter- mination" raid opposite the S.W. Corner of GOMMECOURT Wood. They took 27 slabs of guncotton made up with charge as O.C. 6th Glos. inspectors directed for a large work of madness ascent. Sappers carried out laying of trenches & entering the trench the support Sris was all success opportunity of wrecking, but from the observation of the other party (which got into the trench) it appears that there was been no special	

WAR DIARY or INTELLIGENCE SUMMARY

Army Form C. 2118.

(Erase heading not required.)

Hour, Date, Place	Summary of Events and Information	Remarks and references to Appendices
November		
26th	work of sappers in any case. On that & return the Cheys was brought back. On manner was slightly more U shaped instead of U stranded rather deeply ventilated into bath ine.	
27th	Fort Briggs BRIGGS reported complete	
	Severe frost froze supply pipes by which internments are supplied. Efforts to thaw failed, and supply was carried a few tap in trench supply system close to main tank. The trench supply was from R tank outside pump-head but running was repeated till the thawing was complete.	
28 Sunday	Brigade Change	
29	Thaw. Heavy rain caused increased afternoon	
	Evening working parties much fatigued w/ [?] harapits	
30	Sections no 4 at JATLLY and no 3 HETTENVORDGNE transport	
	& ROSSIGNOL	

W. Gibson Major
O. C. 1st Field Co.
S. Midland R. E.

1st S. MIDLAND FIELD CO.
R.E., T.F.
Date 30/12/15

15ᵗʰ Div 11. s.h. Fr. G. Re.

Dao XII / vol.

Army Form C. 2118.

WAR DIARY
or
INTELLIGENCE SUMMARY
(Erase heading not required.)

Instructions regarding War Diaries and Intelligence Summaries are contained in F.S. Regs., Part II. and the Staff Manual respectively. Title pages will be prepared in manuscript.

Hour, Date, Place	Summary of Events and Information	Remarks and references to Appendices
Dec 1st	Two sections from HEADQUARTERS moved to ROSEL SITE.	
2nd	Loans - Two tips in Camp line chiefly clearing prairie & revetting. One Sec in Bon de BUS. One section on water scheme near COVIN. Details on Billets & Baths	
3rd	As 2nd. Bad weather caused early dismissal of parties	
4th	Bad weather. No Infants parties. Work in Billet	
5th	Working parties as usual. 202nd Coy joined Division	
6th	Brigade Change days. No working parties.	
7th	Sappers clearing up at BUS hard and COTENEUX graves. New graves at COVIN & BUS ended.	Major Cusons went on leave
8th	202 to party started Coy!	
	Work as usual	
9th	Work cancelled for infants parties on acct of weather. Trench across BUS - COVIN road cut & pipe put in for draining water supply. Reinforcement 1 Sec Cpl & 70 men arrived	

WAR DIARY
INTELLIGENCE SUMMARY
(Erase heading not required.)

Army Form C. 2118.

Hour, Date, Place	Summary of Events and Information	Remarks and references to Appendices
Dec 10. 1915	Late start (owing to rain) of wks parties.	Lt Richards promoted to Capt dated 13.11.15
11—13	Work as usual. One party dismissed from work as acct of weather on 13th.	
14th	Bde Change 143rd. Bde went forward 144th back	
15th	Concert held in evening 7 – 9.45 p.m. no working parties of infants. C.O.'s N. work continued	
16	Each Sapper given a day off in one of these days.	
17	Sn 2 & 3 moved 2/Lt HESSOZEARE 3 SAILLY. Remaining J Coy moved to Tete de pte Fd Coy at 142 B. + SAILLY. Dangerous junction Pohnuch Demolishes.	2nd Lt THOMAS slightly wounded. Major CLISSOLD returned from leave.
18	2 & 3rd Fd Cys left HESSOZEARE	
19	Forward Saps started along whole front. 6" Hy J K & 2" H Section	
20	Work as usual. Keep parties on new Intl & Improved If Battalion relies specially asked for by R.E.	
21	Parties on forward Saps cancelled on acct of weather	Lt Strickland went on leave
22	Bde change	

Army Form C. 2118.

WAR DIARY
or
INTELLIGENCE SUMMARY
(Erase heading not required.)

Instructions regarding War Diaries and Intelligence Summaries are contained in F.S. Regs., Part II. and the Staff Manual respectively. Title pages will be prepared in manuscript.

[Stamp: S. MIDLAND FIELD CO. R.E., T.F. 1st. Date......]

Hour, Date, Place	Summary of Events and Information	Remarks and references to Appendices
Dec 23-27/1915	Work on VERCINGETORIX preserved. Revetting on VILLARS carried on as particular. Other works in hand installation of petrol engine to replace engine which broke down on 23rd — erection of sand bag protection for engine — extension of pipe line to junction of VERCINGETORIX–VILLARS & erection of tanks — relaying of REVEL & of dugouts on REMOND BIRON, ALSACE, VILLON LANE & RAYMOND — hanging of Church bell as a gas alarm.	Sapper DOVER wounded
28	Bde Change	
29, 30	Work as before. Construction of new trench latrines DOMINIQUE begun.	
31	Company moves to ROSSIGNOL	

J.T. Cheasure
Major,
O.C. 1st. Field Co.
S. Midland R. E.

1/ S.M. 9a Coy R.E.
Jan / vol. XIII

WAR DIARY or INTELLIGENCE SUMMARY

Army Form C. 2118.

Hour, Date, Place	Summary of Events and Information	Remarks and references to Appendices
Jan 1st 1916	Fatigue for infantry. Work carried on as Cop. line & hurdle making to wood. Map 57D Sq.an J 9 C 29. A screen of brush work was begun at X roads J 15 c 52. Strong of flights carried up J 15 c 77. Sergeant of Horsing the Company had a New Year dinner & smoking concert.	
2nd	Infantry parties stopped by weather. R.E. work on Covin water supply continued.	
3rd	Bargoed Church. R.E. work on screen & wood continued, also at Covin where traverses trough was tipped with metal & 2" pipe laid to waterart supply. Work my parties as usual	
4th	No afternoon work owing to weather. Infantry parties did not arrive till 11½ am owing to weather	
5		
6		
7	Work as usual on Cop. Line, Dugouts, Hurdling.	
8	Bsr. Change. [End to in turn has as ready]	
9	Fat. Say Lt arriving the preceding Bsr Change Special party of 200 R.O.R.L. a fleet ?? two aeroplane trench destroyed at Lovencourt	
10		

WAR DIARY
or
INTELLIGENCE SUMMARY
(Erase heading not required.)

Army Form C. 2118.

Hour, Date, Place	Summary of Events and Information	Remarks and references to Appendices
Jan 11 1916	Pulley for petrol engine at COY HQ ottawa from SM/15M5 & fixed in - trench pump run similar.	
12	Coy moved to HERSUTERNE, no 1 S+ sent to SAILLY. Work in progress - repair of Gas engine, sand bagging Junction Trench, recovery of containers, mattress of VILLARS & reconnaissance dugouts.	
13 } 14 } 15 }	Bent stays (6) boards, pumps with lead. Camouflage experts went on proposed site of Battlen O.P.s. Work begun on six OPs there at K9B52, K10B27, K16C27, K21B02, K21B30. These 8 hrs shift jobs. B50 Change (14th) division ADMA-BIEUX attached by W HORNUNGS. Some work continued.	
15		
16		
18	Pulley obtained for igniter engine at HERSUTERNE & saw installed. Work on dug out + O.P.s continued.	
19.20		
21	Pontoon Change - 145 Bdi came up. Two dud shells exploded in K sector. (Bucks + OXFORDS exchanged sections of) Infantry Part of 25 transferred from VERCHINS & OTTEUX to VILLARS.	
22		
23 24	Work in VILLARS, and OPs OC continued.	

WAR DIARY or INTELLIGENCE SUMMARY

Army Form C. 2118.

1st S. MIDLAND FIELD CO. R.E., T.F.

Hour, Date, Place	Summary of Events and Information	Remarks and references to Appendices
Jan 25/1916	The Company moved to ROSSIGNOL took over Corps line, 3rd took over Strath hutments to COIGNEUX and any first grouping at J 4 a, Erection of cook houses, latrines & ablution sheds.	
26	Work as above	
27	Both changes. No parties on Corps line.	
28	Corps line party, no flint parties hutments	
29	Work as on 26th	
30	Mnto on Road & execution. Withdrawn from Corps Line work. Replaced by 1/5th to party.	Capt Rickard went on leave
31	Company Staff	officers O.R. 6 / 158 } 218
		horses mules 3 / 14
	*includes attached R.A.M.C. 2	Interpreter 1

J Cresson Major
1/1 S.M. F.Cy. R.E.

WAR DIARY
or
INTELLIGENCE SUMMARY

(Erase heading not required.)

Army Form C. 2118.

Hour, Date, Place	Summary of Events and Information	Remarks and references to Appendices
1st February 1916	Company at ROSSIGNOL - work on Corps Lines, huts making in COIGNEUX wood, flint digging, billet repairs & construction of Gas hut at	
2nd	new quarry in COIGNEUX wood. S.B.A. opening	
3rd	Concert by POILUS at ROSSIGNOL - well received	
4th - 5th	Work as usual	
6th	R.E. Stores depot at COIGNEUX - Performance of	
	Cinema	
7 - 8th	Work on Stores & other works as before	9th Lt Thomas went on leave
9th	Cadre training	
10th	Company moved to THEBUTERNE - leaving in 2 S.H. at Reargard and ½ Captain & Interpreter	Capt Richards returned
11	Worked at HEBUTERNE - clearing VAUBAN dr, night, O.P. for "G" off WAGRAM, T.M. dugout off CHAVEZ, brick O.P. off POILUS, dugout off BIRON & GUDIN, institution of Petrol engine & Drawing Station in RUE NEUVE	

48

1/1 S M 7d Coy R.E.
Vol XV

Army Form C. 2118.

WAR DIARY
or
INTELLIGENCE SUMMARY
(Erase heading not required.)

Instructions regarding War Diaries and Intelligence Summaries are contained in F. S. Regs., Part II. and the Staff Manual respectively. Title pages will be prepared in manuscript.

Hour, Date, Place	Summary of Events and Information	Remarks and references to Appendices
12th Feb 1914	Work as on 11th. Pipe in GERTRUDE AVE burst by shell. Water turned off from VERCINGETORIX, but supply in tank lasts till 6.	
13th	Pipe repaired 10 pm — Delay due to alarm & turn out at 1.47 PM.	Lt Roman returns
14th 15th	Work as on 12th	
16th	Worked on M.G. dugout = MARIE LOUISE bypass	
17th 18th	Hot St. changes over, no 2 coming up	
19th 20th	GENEVIEVE O.P.s inner casing begun	Searchlights work in team
21st	Work carried on	
22nd 23rd	O.P. of 16th Siege Bty at WAEREM begun, also M.G. dug out at WAG RAM. Snow. Water supply for Cart. frozen up. Supply continued by hose.	
24	No 3 St. work back no 4 came up.	
25 26	Reinforcement route HERBUTERNE to LASIGNY and SAILLY FLAISGNY marked. RAMC dug out on SAILLY road begun.	

1247 W 3299 200,000 (E) 8/14 J.B.C. & A. Forms/C. 2118/11.

Army Form C. 2118.

WAR DIARY
or
INTELLIGENCE SUMMARY
(Erase heading not required.)

Instructions regarding War Diaries and Intelligence Summaries are contained in F. S. Regs., Part II. and the Staff Manual respectively. Title pages will be prepared in manuscript.

Hour, Date, Place	Summary of Events and Information	Remarks and references to Appendices
Feb 27 1916 28 29	Works carried on. Infants parts 11th nt 15th & 17th On 27th Estimair of Remaus ??? not 17pm  W Cursn Major O.C. 1st Field Co. S. Midland R. E.	

48

1/, S M 2ª Coy R.E.

Vol. 16

WAR DIARY or INTELLIGENCE SUMMARY

Army Form C. 2118.

Hour, Date, Place	Summary of Events and Information	Remarks and references to Appendices
March 1 1916	No1 SK left HERSUZERNE for RINGAZEL Co - changing with no 3 St - Work at ROSSIGNOL yard - work at J 10 c - Chain span in AUTHIE stats work at HERBUTERNE Artilly O.P.s interview Brig nt - Brith O.P. ARTILLEURS - R.A.M.C. Brig M.T.	
2	Reconnoitred O.P.s CARREPL + GENEVIEVE. Brig M.T. BRICKFIELDS. Sharpshooter Farm O.P.work	
3	As above - Snow	
4	Camouflage experts - O.Ps English & French to have English & arrived + set up Tree in MAISON. Snow prevents other camouflages from being finished	
5	Work as in 2, 3. O.P. on MONTAUBIER begun	
6	O.P. 's honorable begun - Camouflages begun in REMAUD, AVERSTADT, PARIN MAISON being overhauled.	2 Lieut Wilson SM from K Company

WAR DIARY or INTELLIGENCE SUMMARY

Army Form C. 2118.

Hour, Date, Place	Summary of Events and Information	Remarks and references to Appendices
March 7-8	Work as on 6th	
9	No 2 section returned to ROSIGNOL replacing No 1	
10-11	Work continued	
12	Bridge O.P. for Gunners finished	
13-15	Work continued	
16	No 4 section to ROSIGNOL	
17	Second shaft in REMOUD O.P. finished	
18	Extension of POILU O.P. begun	
19-20	Work continues. Bomb Steppes in ROSSIGNOL improved	Sapper BOYCE wounded 19th
21	O.P. in KOEVAZLIER finished	
22	Work continued	
23	No 3 section to ROSSIGNOL	
24-26	Camouflage tree in OBSERVATION STREET lowered 3 feet. O.P. in JAREFELD begun	
28	New dugout for 3rd pty begun in MESVEREMD Trench Board for L CARRIERS O.P.	
29	WAGRAM M.G. emplacement finished	
30	No 1 section work on TRENCHNOR CORNAY, EVE Rynh O.P. finishes. Trench board round of MESVERAWS	
31	O.P. in PAPIN enlarged. O.P. in JARFELD finished.	

J.C. Clark
O.C. 1st Midland Field Co.
S. Midland R.E.

WAR DIARY
or
INTELLIGENCE SUMMARY

(Erase heading not required.)

Army Form C. 2118.

Hour, Date, Place	Summary of Events and Information	Remarks and references to Appendices
April 1st 1914		
2-4	The Company less no 1 & 2 Sections, at HEBUTERNE work auto tank posts and M.G. emplacements & work carried on above, also no 1 Sec machine stores at ROSSIGNOL	2 W.O.s Bonne went on leave
5	Pellison M.G. try out hrs	
6	no 2 Sec relieving no 1 at ROSSIGNOL	
7	new work at COIGNEUX hrs	
8,9	work carried on, also preparation for forward dugouts	
	11.00 yards "green" hurt set out in training hrs dawn. Pic no 2 ing to training by parties from Bth & known also wires throughout with 3st kents roots at 3st intervals, & caps being filled with turbid in a sand van posts. The thread now N.att from No 9 Bovillon to PUISIEUX Rd, then supple E of N & round by NNW W to "M" sap, was begun at 8 pm. Parties withdrawn abt 2.45 a.m. Special RE party was made to lay 210yds Junction to PUISIEUX Rd & barricade, and trench for gaps on line.	
11	Several light posts went out in the centre - also 13th & 18th machine	O.C. went on leave
13	Officers men on leave needed to wire	L/Cpl Thomas went sick
14	no 4 Sec went back to ROSSIGNOL - exchanging with no 1	
15	Staff Post & R.A. & PUISIEUX road started	
16		Cpl Hall Hew Commission in San Serv R.F.C.

WAR DIARY
or
INTELLIGENCE SUMMARY
(Erase heading not required.)

Army Form C. 2118.

Hour, Date, Place	Summary of Events and Information	Remarks and references to Appendices
April 18 1916	O.P. to RMA at ABLAIN begun	OC returned from leave
19	Reinforcement of 2 men received also 2 men returned from testing for munitions	
21	No 3 S+ returned to ROSSIGNOL, No 4 came up	
22	PUISIEUX Road O.P. finished	
23	Between COLIN & COIGNEUX No 3 S+ built bridge. Train infants in 4 S. Twin 6 hours, including filling two	
24	French trestles to JONES Bay - marked no previous night	Lieutenant ? went on leave
25	Bryant Avenue	
26	Bde O.P. in JONES begun	
27	Brickfield O.P. finished. Typists? Scandlight? St Vaast Sane	
28	Asslett (parapet) 4.2 / Explosives in Stores, small damage done	
29	The pump by POND in ? failed	
30	Efforts to restore pump - not yet successful	

J.C. Evans
Major
O.C. 1st Field Co
S. Midland R.E.

1247 W 3299 200,000 (E) 8/14 J.B.C. & A. Forms/C. 2118/11.

Army Form C. 2118.

WAR DIARY
or
INTELLIGENCE SUMMARY
(Erase heading not required.)

Vol 7

Hour, Date, Place	Summary of Events and Information	Remarks and references to Appendices
May 1st 1916	The company had 3 Sns at HEBUTERNE one at transport, at ROSSIGNOL. Work 6 hand otst: Pools & cleaning of trenches. Pump by Pond was started again.	
2nd	Pump broken again. Attempt was made to prevent it for phone but it was too deep. A trench at bottom pumped. A sump pit was made & let water strained.	
3rd	The Coy took over trench of No 3 Coy & with no men. The billets at Keep was handed over to 2/1 Leicester F. Coy SB1/4 Sect. and the Coy moved into the "Elephant House" on the CAT MILL Road.	2nd Lt! C.W. Watson joined Coy. Lt. Husband returned from leave.
4	Coy Bridging material sent to them with 3rd FCoy.	
5	2nd Lieut: Brown went to hospital.	
6	Work on Hvy T.M. emplacements & JEAN BART bays	
7	Captain Jeffrey RE.O.P. & Jorvis Strpd b/w of platoon	
9	T.M. Emplacement in CASTRE Starts. New wk	
10	Supply from work in Rue NEUVE going up.	
13	Circular Saw & Rue NEUVE running.	
15	Corps Obs: Post & TUNNEL Trench starts.	
12th	2nd Lieut: Brown returns from Hospital. New circular saw at Rossignol set up.	CSM returns from hospital & has re-enlisting.

Army Form C. 2118.

WAR DIARY
or
INTELLIGENCE SUMMARY
(Erase heading not required.)

Instructions regarding War Diaries and Intelligence Summaries are contained in F. S. Regs., Part II. and the Staff Manual respectively. Title pages will be prepared in manuscript.

1st S. MIDLAND FIELD CO.
R.E. T.F.
Date......

Hour, Date, Place	Summary of Events and Information				Remarks and references to Appendices
May 16th 1916	Work at HEBUTERNE handed over to 3rd N.M. Co. Company marched to ROSSIGNOL				
17					
18	Company marched at 6 am to HEM arrived 11.30 am Training = 6.30 Drill 8.30 – 12 work, 1 – 4 work Programme carried out				
19	No 1 St.	No 2 S/n	No 3 S/n	No 4 S/n	
19	Packing Pontoon Span Bridging	Packing Pontoon Pontoon Bridging	As no 3	As no 1	
20	Span Bridging	Pontoon Bridging Light Bridges	As no 3	As no 1	
21	Swimming	Whipping operays	As no 3	As no 1	
22	Pontooning	Reconnaissance Section & Span Pontoon	As no 3	As no 1	
23	"	Span Bridges	"	Pontoon & Light Bridges	
24	Pontoons & Catamaran (Rafts)	Do. (Rafts)	As no 3	As no 1	
25	Reconnaissance Rowing	Rowing Catamaran	As no & also Trestle Raft		Swimming 8.30 am
26	Pont. & Trestle Bridge Slops 52 min also Repairing Catamaran	As no 1 – 65 min	As no & 65 min	As no 1 80 min	
27	Rowing	Trestle Trestle with ropes on	Raft Pontoon Trestle Pont.	Repair mooring Pontoon Trestle Bridge	
28	Swg & Myht Trestle Pont. Trestle 62 min	As no 2	Night Bridges	As no 3	
29	Musketry	Trestle Bond Pier	Large Pontoon Rafts Night Bridge	Rapid mooring	
30	35 ft Bridge Dropped Trestle	Dropped Trestles Sliders & Spindle	Long supervision Stream = musketry	Demolitions Single Board Rafts	
31	Route march for Kemmels employers on 16" morning Demolitions Musketry		Shocks	Flying Bridge	

1247 W 3299 200,000 (E) 8/14 J.B.C. & A. Forms/C. 2118/11.

48

Army Form C. 2118.

WAR DIARY
INTELLIGENCE SUMMARY
(Erase heading not required.)

Hour, Date, Place	Summary of Events and Information	Remarks and references to Appendices
June 1st 1916	Musketry. Rapid wiring & spars & Hammers. afternoon - Sports.	2nd Lt E.C. Lightner returns from leave
2	Coy moved at 5.20 a.m. to bivouac at 57D J7c35. 1 mile W of SAILLY, transport to ROUGEOT. Sappers arrive 11.10 am. Spent rest of day settling in.	
3	Wore hours 8 a.m. No 3 Sec - Two Sup full day out near GROSVENOR AVE STAD J 3rd Barricade SCARE RD	Capt G. St Richard returns from leave
	2. Two	
	3. Two	
	4. One	
	Details. Two Signal test stations in SAILLY CRUNCAMPS Road Screen on CRUNCAMPS - COVRCOURCE Road Dugout and buildings in The DELL	
	Norm - 3 cylinders & lifts of 4 sappers & 8 infantry in each part of day nts - 3 cylts. - 2 sgts. hour shift of 2 sappers & 6 infy on D'ELL 2 four hour shifts of 2 sappers & 6 infy on Test Stn and one eight hour shift of 1 sapper & 1 off & 40 infy on screen. Works as above continued.	
4, 5, 6	Bthn changed two infy parties from dusk 6/7 to moonlight 7/8	
7	New sig nets & NEW Trench K167c93 begun by No 3 St. which we withdraw from GROSVENOR & a wire part formed by nature	
8	Shifts in AVE STAD & SCARE Rd to 3 sappers without 4.	

WAR DIARY
or
INTELLIGENCE SUMMARY
(Erase heading not required.)

Army Form C. 2118.

Hour, Date, Place	Summary of Events and Information	Remarks and references to Appendices
June 8 1916 (cont)	A new dugout was sited in NEW Trench near PUISIEUX Rd. but could not be begun till approaches were made. Two first parties of 16 knafts were detailed for nos 1 & 4 Sap for carrying on from 9 p.m. to 3 a.m. and a party of 7 to 9 a.m. at same hours for approach in alm.	
9 – 11 p.m.	as 8th	
12 p.m.	as above	
13 p.m.	Parts in approaches to PUISIEUX Rd. Sap not necessary	2 Lt. Lyttleton returns
– 6 a.m.	as above	
	Parts near PUISIEUX Rd. increased to 20/-. Dugout begun	1st 2nd Lt. Wilson went on leave
14 – 18	as above	
19	Bayonets charge – 8 hours infantry party lost	
20	Work continued in Sap entry. with parties still unsatisfactory but made.	
21		
22		
23	Work in Sap not cleared at 4.30 a.m. except for three (blank)	
24	7 shafts only	
	Sap not whence PAPIN carried on under difficulties	
25 – 29	PAPIN. WRANGLE D.O. 14 off. ft 1 flour sharp, passage through. 3rd BARRICADE. Sap not complete but passage but made. DOME – Right 2 Sap not 7 x 4. Left two parts	2nd Lt. Wilson returns
	Occupation by infants. & extreme inefficiency of infantry parties. Drain but near WHITE RES 3 & 5, & various	

Army Form C. 2118.

WAR DIARY
or
INTELLIGENCE SUMMARY
(Erase heading not required.)

Hour, Date, Place	Summary of Events and Information	Remarks and references to Appendices
June 30 1916	In SAILLY - COLINCAMPS - COURCELLES, COLINCAMPS - EXPECIMES and COVR. CE LLES - MAILLY roads repaired. Work on DELL finished. Dumps below DELL formed, and arrangements made for roads forward to be retained on 1/7/16. 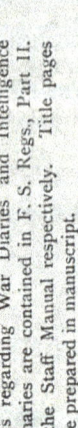 Major. O.C. 1st. Field Co. S. Midland R. E.	

WAR DIARY or INTELLIGENCE SUMMARY

Army Form C. 2118.

Vol 19

Hour, Date, Place	Summary of Events and Information	Remarks and references to Appendices
July 1 1916	Company moved from Bienvillers near SAILLY to BIENVILLERS S.W. of MAILLY-MAILLET having potions trenches with barbed wire at ROSIGNOL	
2	Company rests in billets. Some reconnaissance work. Major, Party J no 2 S's went out to tape & stake lines for 14.5" R.H. attack at 10.30pm but open was unexpected when they reached MESNIL	
3	Further Officers' Reconnaissance. Coy returned to Bienvillers Inde W. of SAILLY in the evening	
4	Roads cleaning. Repaired drill etc. Lt Lightbody & 20 men sent to HEBUTERNE still attached to relieve party J 2 W.R. Coy. Took over line PUISIEUX Rd to TOUTVENT where starts at 17:25 and DELL.	
5	Began dugouts with corrugated iron & under houses in Rue Neuve. Repaired between SAILLY- COURCELLES Rd.	
6	Q 5th.	
7	Q 5th. 2 H night attempts to lay out new trench SERRE Rd to PUISIEUX Rd. No sufficient time	
8	New trench laid out. 204th Coy arrives Bienvillers	

Army Form C. 2118.

WAR DIARY
or
INTELLIGENCE SUMMARY
(Erase heading not required.)

S. MIDLAND FIELD CO. R.E. T.F.

Hour, Date, Place	Summary of Events and Information	Remarks and references to Appendices
July 9 1916	2o & 1st F.d Cy. handed over work in cellars HEBUTERNE continued	
10	at night. Opn 740X from x 5 for to taken from of new trench K17 c 51 to K17 a 26 with 3 communication trenches from french front line.	
11 – 13	Work as on 9th. New trench dug by Oxford & Bucks at night. Parties placed in work only by R.E.	
14	Work in cellars. Three of these finished. Orders to toms by hmr Scott. Work suspended. 12th Fd Cy. arrived ← Bienvue. 2nd Fd Cy. handed	
15	over Stores at ROSSIGNOL, jumpo oc & 9th Fd Cy. H.Q. & Sec 2 & 3 moved to Bienvue at W13 a 45. Remainder of 2nd Fd. Co. F ROSSIGNOL – 124th Cy. showr round. Party Officers NCOs & men reconnoitring new front in OVILLERS.	
~~15~~ 16	HEBUTERNE section handed over to 1/2 Fd Cy. Start 7/23 Reconnaissance E & ALBERT toward LA BOISELLE and CRI at OVILLERS.	
17	Further reconnaissance for CRE at OVILLERS. One section on Stores at BOUZINCOURT. Capt Richard & Sec 2 & 3 moved to BOUZINCOURT. One section on Stores. Reconnaissance of BOUZINCOURT water supply	

WAR DIARY or INTELLIGENCE SUMMARY

Army Form C. 2118.

Hour, Date, Place	Summary of Events and Information	Remarks and references to Appendices
July 21, 1916	Infantry track from BOIZINCOURT to BOUZINCY, & supports forward. Junction of track L x 3d old 270° dug by no 28 & 1 x Coy officer Pioneers. Work delayed by heavy shelling. Reconnaissance continued. Infantry track completed.	Casualties (signs) Sapper Richards R3 Plater PH Norman JJ Wright JA Crean JR Beer L
22	(6 men 7 no 1 s²) Trench F 93 t 28 dug 3' wide average 3' deep by sappers & no 1 & 2 Coys. Strongpoint at point 11 begun by no 3 sect Eng.	
23	Reconnaissance of points 5th proceeding. Strong points continued at pt 11 & no 4 s² at pt 81 by no 1 s².	Casualties LaCpl Reeve Sapper Rogers
24	East of Pt 87 fort. Company moved to Bouzincourt. Track from AVELUY to ALBERT road. Strongpoints 11 & 87 continued by no 4 & 1 Coys and point 28 begun for one. Very little can be done at either point owing to large estab² of infantry ready for attack & at pt 28 in that it will not now be one.	

WAR DIARY or INTELLIGENCE SUMMARY

Army Form C. 2118.

Hour, Date, Place	Summary of Events and Information	Remarks and references to Appendices
July 18 1916	Report on Road Reconnaissance OVILLERS & MASH VALLEY SHELTERS. Repair of roads to Church BOUZINCOURT. New water cart supply begun. New trenches dug in W of POZIÈRES, one a depth of 3 ft 6 ins not. Work on store BOUZINCOURT	
19	Work on stores - water cart supply finished - storage tank erected on BAPAUME road W of BOUZINCOURT. Trench to front of POZIÈRES deepened - new trench to depth 3'0" South of BAPAUME road begun. Work under interference with	Casualties - Cpl Hallett severe Serjeant Lee slight Sapper Padfield "Martin "
20	gas shells & shrapnel - 4 casualties. Work in stores - 40 gal tank erected opposite BOUZINCOURT at X13 d 11. Trench to Corps Signal X9a66 - X8a70 started. Work further interfered with by shrapnel + [illumination?] shells) by no 1 Sec with 1000 infants. Trench 6 x 9 1/2 x 5 N.W. [clumm?] of first by no 4 Sec.	
21	Comm. [bttn?] trench at La BOISSELLE established in Inf- unt at La BOISSELLE at X14c 70 65 and X13a 73 Reconnaissance carried out of (a) communication to/8 from AVELUY + USNA (b) dugouts in OVILLERS KEEP & Junction OVILLERS (c) comm trench from OS KSI (d)	Casualties - Supplementary

WAR DIARY or INTELLIGENCE SUMMARY

Army Form C. 2118.

Hour, Date, Place	Summary of Events and Information	Remarks and references to Appendices
July 26 1916	Our front B9 hours his captive as I am afraid under NF have been interior (in spite of arrangement made with Brigadier) a party was sent up at 5 a.m. to resuscitate. The party marched 11-89 at 9 p.m. on what too 1 p.m. Reconnaissance of dry outposts finished. Report in AVENUE STREET nomenclature sent in to O.C. R.E. at night. Fatigue party to complete strong points and deepen communication trench to C.28. Whilst carrying stores they came under shell fire. 1st shell was at our post on west - 40 yds in rear here fatigued, including 2nd Lt. Browne. Officers 2nd Lt Browne & 35 O.R. was detained at First Aid. Work was stopped. Work on communication trench to C.28 carried on & finished.	Casualty Supper Hole
27		
28	Day on night of 27/m worked as on night of 27/28 - Report on day work accommodation sent in to CRE - heir by 2345 Light Ry Wilson & Watson /QD new trench parallel to the BAPAUME road to walk 9 ft 900' long was begun with a fatigue of 5th R. Sussex //. This trench was carried on. Only two hours work was done. G. was under orders of CRE 12 Div.	2nd Lt Browne Sergt Hill Cpl Mitchell 2 Cpl Brown 1 Sapper + 36 O.R. injured
29		
31		

WAR DIARY or INTELLIGENCE SUMMARY

Army Form C. 2118.

(Erase heading not required.)

Hour, Date, Place	Summary of Events and Information	Remarks and references to Appendices
July 29th 1916	Coy moved by motor-bus from BOUZINCOURT to DOMQUEUR, marching to BOUZINCOURT + entraining at 4.40 pm. Transport moved under Capt Richards to TALMAS. 2 lorries to transport ran via R.E. stores re. hike from in ALBERT. Cyclists moved to TALMAS.	
July 30th	Church Parade at PLOUY 10.30 am. Transport reaches DOMQUEUR at 2 pm. + Cyclists about noon. Parade 5.30 am. — R.E. store started — work for Bath. Tent making — repair of harness-watering appts. Morning parade musketry & semaphore.	
July 31st		

J.T. Churchin

O.C. 1st Midland Field Co. R.E.

48th Divisional Engineers

1/1st SOUTH MIDLAND FIELD COMPANY R.E.

AUGUST 1 9 1 6 :::::

Army Form C. 2118.

WAR DIARY
or
INTELLIGENCE SUMMARY
(Erase heading not required.)

Instructions regarding War Diaries and Intelligence Summaries are contained in F. S. Regs, Part II. and the Staff Manual respectively. Title pages will be prepared in manuscript.

Hour, Date, Place	Summary of Events and Information	Remarks and references to Appendices
August 1st 1916	Re Company at DOMQUEUR - work - troops making training repairs. Draining & spalls breaking. Also was jumble whites.	Lt Barratt joins Coy
2nd	As on 1st.	
3rd - 5th	A 3rd Coy moved to ST ETOILE for pontooning practice which was carried out at 5 am - 11 am & other Coys assisting. Equipment taken to St & St ... and 5 am to 10 am on the 5th. At 3 pm Coy returned to DOMQUEUR	Reinforcement of 1 NCO & 29 men arrives at DOMQUEUR.
7th	Several Officers went to CAYEUX for the day. A party of Sappers & NCOs went to ABBEVILLE. Remainder musketry signalling.	
8th 12th	Sunday - Church Parade PLOUY. Parts of NCOs & 2nd Lts King joins Coy went to ABBEVILLE.	
8	Coy moved to LONGVILLERS - Bivouacked	
9	marched to AUTHEULE - Bivouacked. Draft 10th & 2nd Lt Barrett exchange with 2nd Lt Nielson Parties of Sappers & Drivers went to ACHEUX - BUS

Army Form C. 2118.

WAR DIARY
or
INTELLIGENCE SUMMARY
(Erase heading not required.)

Instructions regarding War Diaries and Intelligence Summaries are contained in F. S. Regs., Part II. and the Staff Manual respectively. Title pages will be prepared in manuscript.

Hour, Date, Place	Summary of Events and Information	Remarks and references to Appendices
11 Aug 1916	Coy remains at ACHEUX	
12 "	do. Drills in continuous mining. Drafting?	
13 "	2 disposed? storm? limes to bivouac at AVELUY. 2d Lieutenant two guns two limbers to day out at RUBBLE STREET. Transport at BOUZINCOURT. Night 13/14 Two F.O.O's intermediate position 1 & 3 to SKYLINE Trench. Work wiring on storm point & RATION Trench "in conjunction with O.C. 8th Lancashire" a O.C. took no interest in them they were not begun. Report in helin 9 storm pnt? behind our premises.	
14	Bivouac formed at 79 & nr 1 & 3 Brs. Work on NEW Trench & TANK by Lieut stopped by slab fire F.O.O. & SKYLINE	207 J. King wounded at OVILLERS
15	Work on storm point 11, 5&, 89, 91 by Sny 1 & 2 & RATION Trench storm points by Sny 3 & 4. Nos 1 & 3 Sn storm points mis SKYLINE?, S˙2 out?!! S˙4 forming Dump with help? parts.	4 Cpl Mitchell C,S,W at Bt Sapper Blythe wounded Hawthorn evening Sapper Davis S W at Bt instead " at Dt Tucker " " at Bt
16		
17	h & S. RATION Trench, Nos 2, 5: NEW Trench & 7 SKYLINE Nos 4 Dump at 68	2 Cpl Lewis W Enr Ib? Thorne S W at Dt

WAR DIARY or INTELLIGENCE SUMMARY

Army Form C. 2118.

Hour, Date, Place	Summary of Events and Information	Remarks and references to Appendices
18 Aug 1916	1 O.C. as usual. No. 1 Sec. M.G. Posts Nethostrench, No 3 Sec on RATION No. 1 constructing 88 - No 2 mtce. Sec. charge on Litanus Brunner & dug outs.	Draftly Stm arrived. Sapper Bishop wounded.
19 Aug	Nos 2 & 3 Secs with 20 v infantry dug new P.J. blown. Nos 1 & 4 mtce. RATION & SKYLINE.	Sapper Crosse RE. died of wounds.
20	Work on new trench from BERMSTRASSE to P.T. 99 & completion of P.T. shed up R SKY LINE. + Sapper wounded returns to duty.	Sapper Jeansparry wounded. Bulcher RA wounded. Sapper W.S. at duty.
21	No. 1 S.T. wt. 700 infty wrkd at Trench - R33c. No 3 S. with No 2 of Sec met to Leipzig Redoubt & clear 2 up ps C who were evacuating X 12.19. One it was known from to constrct R 31 d 81 but it was too dark. Nos 2 o 4 Sec clock by	Sapper Hamilton woundeded.
22	Nos 2 o 4 Secs clock by No 1 & 3 wrks on trenches R 33 c. with infty parts 170 v.	S/Lt Sm Wilson wounded. Sapper Hamer wounded, lift at duty.
23	Nos 2 & 4 Sec worked on a new strong point at R33 c 68, & No 3 S. on point near 14 left in SKYLINE trench. No. 1 Cpl Homily. Sec carried on opening up communication between X 26-59	L/Corpt wounded. Corpl Sutherland wounded Sept 6 & 16. Cpl homily. Sapper Laws. Batteries 65.
24	& 48 & X 2 a 79. with 200 infantry. Strong point R 33 c 68 continued. 200 wire fence exprm Post inft. Strong point R 33 c 14 nearly finished. wire down in trenches X 12 59 - 48 - a 79.	Sapper English wounded. Rogers wounded.

WAR DIARY or INTELLIGENCE SUMMARY

Army Form C. 2118.

Hour, Date, Place	Summary of Events and Information	Remarks and references to Appendices
Aug 25 1916	Trench X26 97-59 (Cleared) - work with wire parties	
26	No 1 & 4 sections with 5th Sussex worked at Stirring Point in SULPHUR	L.Cpl Browning wounded
	Avenue at X 32.71 & X 3-40. Nos 2 & 3 Secs with 6/15 Warwick parties worked at clearing 6th, 7th & 8th Street. Took on 6th Street trench interfered with shelling. Pumps taken over from No 3.5 Section. No pumps at work & No 106 P² Coy. No 2 Section under 2nd Lieut. Struth assisted 145th Bn ↓ 13 on prog ↑ Ken Attack by excavating & making M G emplacement & communication trench. No 3	
27	Section under 2 Lt Watson detailed to No 3 Bn were part of No 145 Bn & assisted 4th Bn to 24 hrs Comm. trench & captured position. A company (70 strong) of 5th Sussex were employed between there & trains. Coy moved to hut at BUS Chateau starting 7.30 am. The three Secs Nos 2 & 3 followed at 2 pm	2/Lt Watson returned
28		

Army Form C. 2118.

WAR DIARY
or
INTELLIGENCE SUMMARY

(Erase heading not required.)

Hour, Date, Place	Summary of Events and Information	Remarks and references to Appendices
Aug 29 1916	Coy rested in bivouac; work on pumps; bath house & Divl Canteen also on Div HQ.	
30	Work on above; Kit inspection; work on water raising plant	
31	Work as above	

W Chard
Major
O.C. 1st Field Co.
S. Midland R.E.

48th. DIVISIONAL ENGINEERS

1/1st. S. M. FIELD COY. ROYAL ENGINEERS

SEPTEMBER 1916.

Vol 21

Confidential
War Diary
of
1/1st S.M. Field Coy R.E. 48th Divn.
From 1st Sept. 1916 to 30th Sept. 1916.

Army Form C. 2118.

WAR DIARY
or
INTELLIGENCE SUMMARY
(Erase heading not required.)

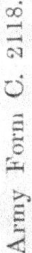

Hour, Date, Place	Summary of Events and Information	Remarks and references to Appendices
1st September 1916	Coy at BUS-les-ARTOIS - Bayonet Drill & morning - work on pumps & transport wash - water pump appts.	
2nd	Drill - Canteen - baths - staff for curio - door H.Q.	
3rd	Coy drill & morning - work for G.O.C. appts. Inspection by G.O.C. - work for Curio - water rain Mass of Junior mens.	2 Lt. C.J. Cooper joined Coy
4th, 5th	Coy parade - 2 Lt. Browne went to Amiens 5th	
6th	Coy practice adv from Square	
7th	Coy drill	
8th	Restaurant. Experiments with water raising appls.	
9th	Musketry - arms drill. O.C. went to Amiens	
10th	Church Parade - Musketry - experiments water raising	
11	Company moved to LONGUEVILLETTE. Water raising appts. on this bit especially not sufficiently powerful for 160ft well	
12	Coy at Longuevillette - Lectures by O.C. & Adv. 5s. ruatpents	
13	Coy moved to HEM	
14	ho 1 St Bridging - Revision drill & musketry of knotting & lashing	
15	ho 2 St Bridge - Revision. Baths at GEZAINCOURT - musketry knotting & lashing	

Army Form C. 2118.

WAR DIARY
or
INTELLIGENCE SUMMARY
(Erase heading not required.)

Instructions regarding War Diaries and Intelligence Summaries are contained in F. S. Regs, Part II. and the Staff Manual respectively. Title pages will be prepared in manuscript.

Hour, Date, Place	Summary of Events and Information	Remarks and references to Appendices
Sept 16 1916	Bath at Bequicourt – Musketry – Knotting lashing	
17	No 3 Sec Bridging	
18	No 4 Sec Bridging – remainder wiring musketry	
19	Coy went OCCOCHES Drill & musketry – lecture & Gas lecture & CSE	
20	bee of instrument for NCOs – Route march & Sappers	
21	Inoculation of men not inoculated with TAHS. Drill & musketry – Boat throwing	
22	musketry – Sappers & half Sec Drivers – water raising plant	
23	Set up at BERNAVILLE & experiments with all 115" trestle	
	Coy went to CANDAS. water plant works at BERNAVILLE	
24–28	water plant worked continuously about 2500 gals. daily	
	(max obtained 3100). Musketry at range 1 mile W of BEAU-	28th
	VAL Church reconnaissance; field observation; inspection of	Lieuts Hamilton and Luiputn on leave
	Baths at Candas. 27th Royaleu Dove Innes with Offr Staff/17th	
29	Coy went to SOMEREN with 145 Bde	
30	Coy went to SOMEREN Hd – Football match aged A+C N.Mid Div Renft. 5–0 agst. Gas lecture – interim Gas	

J.S. Chiesman
Major

Vol 22

Confidential.

War Diary
of 2nd/1st South Mid Cand Field Co RE
48th Division
From 1st October 1916 to 31st October 1916

Army Form C. 2118.

WAR DIARY
or
INTELLIGENCE SUMMARY
(Erase heading not required.)

Instructions regarding War Diaries and Intelligence Summaries are contained in F. S. Regs., Part II. and the Staff Manual respectively. Title pages will be prepared in manuscript.

Hour, Date, Place	Summary of Events and Information	Remarks and references to Appendices
1 Sept 1916	Coy moved to GAUDIEMPRE. Detachment 3 Carpenters, 1 Plumber, 1 Fitter, 2 Engine Drivers sent to CRG at HENU, also water Sun party.	2nd Lt Nicholls Clarke joined Company
2	Work on Baths at HENU, improved entry to have lines. A list of Honours gained by H.Coy was made out. It contains –	
	– 5 . 15 Major E Gardiner D.S.O.	
	– 11 . 15 488 Sapt Denham A } Green Card – recognition	
	1319 Cpl Capel A C } by 48th Div Comdr.	
	960 Spr Harding B	
	693 Sapt Hoof pro H.J.	
	12.15 960 Spr Harding A. mentioned in Despatches	
	14.1.16 488 Sapt Denham A } D.C.M.	
	1319 Cpl Capel A C }	
	3 . 6 . 16 Major H. Clavicord D.S.O.	
	24 . 8 . 16 600 Cpl Mitchell D J M.M.	
	29 . 8 . 16 Capt E&A Richard M C	
	30 . 8 . 16 839 Sapper Edmond A E D.C.M.	
	11 . 9 . 16 1576 2nd Cpl Mitchell C } M.M.	
	1359 L/Cpl Lockspeiser L }	
	15 . 9 . 16 Lieut H.W.T. Husbands M.C.	
3	Secs 1 & 2 sent to FONCQUEVILLERS. Very wet day. – Drill & afternoon of 3 & 4 Secs – work on pump.	

WAR DIARY or INTELLIGENCE SUMMARY

Army Form C. 2118.

Hour, Date, Place	Summary of Events and Information	Remarks and references to Appendices
Oct 4	Sappers moved to LA HAYE Sec 1 & 2 covering both front of QUESNOY VILLERS. 12 men reconnu at HERRU with CRE. Stores at HQRS taken over from 2 W.R. Coy. Recon & inspection in relation between SOUASTRE & ROSSIGNOL FARM on repairs to dug outs at LA HAYE – Conference with Brigadier 143.	
5	9th Day – Reconnaissance 2 Coys. Shrapnel (A & C) attached for work. 2 Coys Booker 156 at HQRS also available. Stores started at CAT MILL & BLUFF DUMP. No new avalanche tcat Irerland Trench BLUFF – CAT starts.	
6	HQR sheets to SOUASTRE. Coy. inspections at LA HAYE – working daily with an average of 300 inf + 2 Coys S.R.E sappers. Work includes re-construction of all trenches B & D E between YUSSIF & YANKEE cutting a connection between A & B near Pylat in 7 2 ridges. Construction of (new) dumps in YOUNG & YELLOW and filling them from CAT MILL – carrying BLUFF & CAT MILL laying track, subsequent removal and lain thro' VALLEY Trench to FORT DICK, thence by short new trench to VALLEY & along Railway Track toward LA HAYE – straightening YIDDISH – cutting off corner from NOTT to TOZPE STAND	
7—17		

WAR DIARY or INTELLIGENCE SUMMARY

Army Form C. 2118.

Hour, Date, Place	Summary of Events and Information	Remarks and references to Appendices
Oct 7-17	Offs out - cutting them for SAFETY EVANS & YOUNG - permanent ladders in YOUNG YIDDISH & YELLOW - putting up trench constants. Beylum stn at CAT ALLE - advanced dummy sisters at SORTESPRO (unfinished - abandoned) - O.P. at junction of YELLOW & R - dam in f [?] near YOUNG - counter YIDDISH - repairs to T.M. emplacements nr YOUNG - construction of advanced H.Q. of Bn. at LA HAIE SAIE building & repairs of cart dry outs, boarding & furnishing others - Construction of a new me (unfinished) - running railway from LA HAIE to BAYENCOURT & relaying LA HAIE - SORTESPRO rmd. Abt 15 sappers on details all the time treated at new hutment camp in carpenters work - hut creation - erection of new hut-shelter ˢC 9 new hut-shelter ˢC standard nos work to 3ᴼ & nrᵗ Cₒ, & to our WHISKEY FRANCIS incluries 9 standing nos to WIRE RD by Cₒ marches for La HAIE Football match Bart head Offrs vs Sgts by 5-0 marched to PERNOIS - unlimbered for 130 men " Talmas	L Wᵐ Brown went on leave

Army Form C. 2118.

WAR DIARY
or
INTELLIGENCE SUMMARY
(Erase heading not required.)

Instructions regarding War Diaries and Intelligence Summaries are contained in F.S. Regs., Part II. and the Staff Manual respectively. Title pages will be prepared in manuscript.

Hour, Date, Place	Summary of Events and Information	Remarks and references to Appendices
24 Nov 1916	marched to LA HOUSSOYE — 2nd billet lot crowded	
25	" ALBERT	
26	Nos 1 & 2 Sens to FRICOURT FARM	
28	Coy moved to CONTALMAISON CUTTING — huts to came in it	
	FRICOURT FARM	
29 – 31	took in Roads BAZENTIN HILL & BAZENTIN — MARTINPUICH. Weather has been fine of late & roads almost impassable. It seems that the Division is fine to throw has been allowed to rest & altogether is for some time without large maintenance parties. no metal available only debris of huts &c	

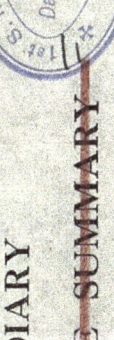

Condg. 1/1 South Midland Field Coy RE (T.F.)

J Chievren
maji

Vol 23

Confidential.
War Diary
of
1/1st South Midland Field Company R.E.
48th Division.
From 1st November 1916. — 30th November 1916.

WAR DIARY or INTELLIGENCE SUMMARY

Army Form C. 2118.

Hour, Date, Place	Summary of Events and Information	Remarks and references to Appendices
1 November 1916	Coy at CONTALMAISON, attd to FREICOURT PATROL	
2 – 4	3 Sections Nos 1, 3, 4 moved to MARTINPUICH area in from 2 pm of 7th Div G.C.	
	Work – improvement of communication trenches – formation of WEST END DUMP MARTINPUICH – cleaning gunpits & repair of dug outs – Bde 2 Drill Baths – Corduroy road on BAZENTIN	
	1744 – Road reclamation BAZENTIN – MARTINPUICH – Tramway E of GUNPIT Road	
5	50th Sec took the BUTTE at 9 am – Others to SUE & by tunnel through hands with them. 2 SOx run by when it was found that no one was with it enemy who had retaken the BUTTE.	2nd/Sapper HAMILTON G slightly wounded
	At 2 am – Lt Wale in wire hands over to Strenue of the Hants new work in Rgt Sub Area to gripfith	all return within hour
6 – 8		
9, 10	1st Lt Stennette went up to M-CH	
11	2nd Lt Mitchell Clarke went to M-CH.	2nd Lt Mitchell Clarke [killed?]
12	Section changes over between M-CH & BAZENTIN camp shown	Sergt Grindt Killed
	shelling at M-CH.	L/Cpl Reeve Sapper A Hanna severely wounded (Abbeville hospital 14)

Army Form C. 2118.

WAR DIARY
or
INTELLIGENCE SUMMARY

(Erase heading not required.)

Instructions regarding War Diaries and Intelligence Summaries are contained in F.S. Regs., Part II. and the Staff Manual respectively. Title pages will be prepared in manuscript.

Hour, Date, Place	Summary of Events and Information	Remarks and references to Appendices
13 November 1916	Work-hard - Clearing up of GILBERT ALLEY, 20 dug outs in O.G.1, O.P. near MILL, formation of WEST END DUMP. Dug out in BAPAUME RD. - Dug out at LESARS (12 tunnellers supplied by 185th Cy.). - Bri Baths near MAMETZ WOOD	
14 - 27th St.	As above - 12 mm tunnellers arrived on 16th - on 18th and 19th Divs on railway GUNPIT RD to LESARS stopped & 4 tunnellers to Second Army M-CH	2nd Lt Watson returned from leave
	Circular saw started at MARTINPUICH Section at MARTINPUICH returned. 2nd Lt Sinclair took off P.O.D. to live in Sunken Road LE SARS. Div7 took over further Section to Right. St 7 No 3 Cy. Sent up more hos Cy. to MARTINPUICH F.O.O. LE SARS returned	Interpreter invalided to hospital Sapper Walker wounded
21st 23rd 24th 25th 28th 30th	Reinforcements arriving Kraut Rejoined unit 4th 1 12th 1 15th 6 15th 1 22nd 5 23rd 1 30th 2	JMClean Dr

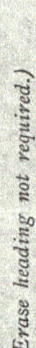

Vol 24

CONFIDENTIAL.

WAR DIARY

of

1/1st (S.M.) FIELD COMPANY R.E.

From 1st Dece,ber 1916 ......to......31st December 1916.

Army Form C. 2118.

WAR DIARY
INTELLIGENCE SUMMARY
(Erase heading not required.)

Hour, Date, Place	Summary of Events and Information	Remarks and references to Appendices
Dec 1st 1916	Transport at FRICOURT FARM, HQrs + 2 Sec at BAZENTIN CAMP, 2 Sec (with nucleus of No 3 Cy attached) at MARTINPUICH, F.O.O. at the SPURS (2 × 1 Corpn) F.O.O. 2nd Lt Sinclair relieves 2nd Lt Cooper	
2		
3	Nos 2 + 3 Sec relieve No 1 Sec at MARTINPUICH. O.C. put up to M-CH.	
4	New Trench Tram Starts for SPRS MULE CORNER to New Trenches near Starts to SPRS MULE CORNER to prepare attack postponed OC returns to Bazentin [or returns to BAZENTIN]	2nd Lt SKINNER joins Cy.
5	Tail Rons. O.P. line & CRESCENT ALLEY being typed F.O. returns	
6	Day out with parties out to TUNNELLING COY (250)	
8	F.O. brought back from Bazentin	
9	Section Reliefs - wiring begun on gap between	
10	MAXWELL & SPUR, later left for SPUR & BAZENTIN Road	Cpl Clements recommended (1112)
11-13	Wiring trench system in GILBERT	
14	Handed over to 74th Fd 91st Fd Cos	
15	Sappers moved from BAZENTIN No 1 Sec & FRICOURT remainder to SHELTER WOOD NORTH. Sackburpe Camp with 2nd Sheps Co. Took no work from 9th Gordons - erection of Messen huts at X22 b 6 and X 22 b 7. Began moving camp	

WAR DIARY
or
INTELLIGENCE SUMMARY

Army Form C. 2118.

Hour, Date, Place	Summary of Events and Information	Remarks and references to Appendices
16	from SUZANNE hutting NORTH to FRICOURT. 3 hutting parties (RA) on above - shus completion? 3 tonnent HUTS at X.20.b.91	
17	Work as above. No. 4 Sec. moved to FRICOURT FROM. No. 2 to their hut at X.19.b.09	Major H. Clissold went on leave.
18	Work as above. Major H. Clissold returned Div School of Instruction	
19	Work as above	
20	H.Q. moved to FRICOURT FARM Camp X.28.c.55. Work as above. 3 hut huts at X.19.b.07. Finished & work started on 5 more NISSEN huts at X.15.d.91	
21	as above	
22		
23	Work as above. Gas School hut etc. & Incinerator photo started at X.28.c.24	In Bn camps
24	Work as above. No. 3 Section moved to Somm. Le Cab HAYES	
25	Went to England. Matt & vino to reunion a communion. Xmas Day. Church Parade. Holiday & Company Dinner	
26	Work as above. Decauville track taken over from 1/2 SMO & RE running from BAZENTIN Road to X.23.c. & fuel camps there. Work stopped on RA. NISSEN Huts until further of materials	
27-28	as above	
29	YMCA hut taken over from 281 AT Coy RE at BECOURT CAMP. RE for C.C.S. reconstituted with S.O. III Corps RE	2/Lt D M WILSON went on leave

WAR DIARY
or
INTELLIGENCE SUMMARY

Army Form C. 2118.

Hour, Date, Place	Summary of Events and Information	Remarks and references to Appendices
Jan 1915		
30	Work as above	2Lt C.M Watson went on Course at Div School
31	Work as above. Work handed over during day to 1/2 SM D/GRE St. GRATIEN.	

Pa Richards
Capt.
for O.C. 1/1 S.M. 2d Coy R.E.
31/1/15

Vol 25

CONFIDENTIAL.

WAR DIARY

of

1/1st. (South Midland) Field Company, R.E.

from 1st January 1917........to........31st January 1917.

Army Form C. 2118.

WAR DIARY
or
INTELLIGENCE SUMMARY

(Erase heading not required.)

Hour, Date, Place	Summary of Events and Information	Remarks and references to Appendices
1st January 1917.	Company mustered C.R.E III Corps for work on	2nd Lt. Sinclair went on leave.
	3 Section arrived as new road his alleged Decauville track	
	as above. 12 Carpenters reported to "G" Dump to work on proposed huts.	
2.	2 Section as above - 1 Section on YMCA hut X21.G.	
3.		
4.	2 Sections this morn stock track at E.11.d.85. as the section was standing.	
	1 Section on YMCA hut X21.G.	
5.	2 Sections loaded up materials at E.11.d into lorries of Sectiion YMCA hut X21.G	
	Also prepared branch line necessitated from La BOISELLE to Chapes Spur.	
	Company transferred to work to CRE 15th Div	
6.	1 Section branchline La BOISELLE - Chapes Spur. 1 Section YMCA hut X21.G.	
7.	1 Section YMCA hut BECOURT, ½ Section attached to 15th Div Tram for	(taken over from ½ SM 3rd C.R.E.
	work on horse standings. and 1 section YMCA hut at X21.G.	
	also instruction received from Corps to mark parts which were	
	running to YMCA hut at "G" Dump. Work for gas school on	
	incinerator sheds in Camps at X21.G.	
8.	as above	
	4 Carpenters sent to "G" dump for work on parts for YMCA hut.	2nd Lt ? Ham to work on leave
9.	as above & also Nissen huts at S7d85.	
10.	as above	
11.	as above and foot inspection finishes in Camp of all Inf Units.	

WAR DIARY
or
INTELLIGENCE SUMMARY

Army Form C. 2118.

Hour, Date, Place	Summary of Events and Information	Remarks and references to Appendices
12 Jan 1917	On G.H.R.	
13th	No stunt. BYMCA BECOURT finished. Also YMCA x 216 ready for cement party, but not completed. All work handed over to 73rd 3rd A.R.E. Orders received in evening for Company to move to relieve 36 Coy of 33rd Division at FLEXICOURT & PONT REMY.	Major Clinrole d/CRE 48th Div. visited Coy.
14	Moved HQ + 3 sections by bus to PONT REMY + 1 section to FLEXICOURT. Transport by road to BEAUCOURT.	
15	Took over work from 11th Inf Coy RE. on 1st Army Musketry Camp Transport moved to FLEXICOURT.	2nd Lt Cooper went on leave
16	Work on Range. Constructing into galley Range. With French for makers in Trainabout ground of PONT REMY. Work on Range & 330 yds to PONT REMY. COQUEREL & FRANCIERES.	Major Clinrole returned to Company.
17	Coy visited St at FLEXICOURT	
18	Work at COQUEREL & FRANCIERES discontinued to concentrate on Range.	2nd Lt Sinclair proceeded for leave 2nd Lt Watson ?
19	Major Clinrole went to 4th Army School of Instruction at La Parroy for a C.O's course. 2nd Lt P.H. Brown left in charge of Company. No. 3 Section working on Range at Z bult digging gallery for markers No. 4 Section working in French carpentry shops. No. 2 Section on various jobs about Pont Remy. No. 1 Section remains at FLEXICOURT under orders from 1st Army School	Capt Pritchard went on leave

Army Form C. 2118.

WAR DIARY
or
INTELLIGENCE SUMMARY
(Erase heading not required.)

Instructions regarding War Diaries and Intelligence Summaries are contained in F. S. Regs., Part II. and the Staff Manual respectively. Title pages will be prepared in manuscript.

Hour, Date, Place	Summary of Events and Information	Remarks and references to Appendices
Jan 1917		
21	Range closed for 3 days to Sappers to allow of shortening some of the 3 action in adjs.	
22	Work same as yesterday.	
23	General and re-enlisted as arrival. Began two latrines area	
24	Two Kitcheners, canvas room eng. Completed yesterday's work. 4 Sappers who have been detached for work on Bhogirit Camp returned to Company.	
25	Revetting of Range Gallery began. Lieutenant B. de Frontball's returned from leave. 2nd Lt Hunter returned from leave.	
26	A man was evacuated to mobile VI Section at Fontaine au Somme. 2nd Lt Adams took over the work at Pont-Remy on behalf of 73rd Field Co RE and then returned to his Company.	
27	Moved Company to agreement arrival 5:30pm. Sapper Sale fell sick was evacuated by RAMC at Hiercourt to CCS. Picked up 421 Section under Lt Fisher at Hiercourt	

1747 W 3299 200,000 (E) 8/14 J.B.C. & A. Forms/C. 2118/11.

Army Form C. 2118.

WAR DIARY
or
INTELLIGENCE SUMMARY
(Erase heading not required.)

Instructions regarding War Diaries and Intelligence Summaries are contained in F. S. Regs., Part II. and the Staff Manual respectively. Title pages will be prepared in manuscript.

Hour, Date, Place	Summary of Events and Information	Remarks and references to Appendices
Jan 28th 29th	Arrived Company at 10.26am to Aubigny, arrived 3.15pm. Company left at 10am and reached Hamel at noon when the 143rd Bde joined us.	
30 31	Nothing to note. Company at Hamel.	

Sh. Brown major.
for O.C.
4th Field Co RE

Vol 26

C O N F I D E N T I A L.
****
W A R   D I A R Y

of

474th (S.M.) Field Company R.E.

From 1st February 1917..........to...........28th February 1917.

Army Form C. 2118.

WAR DIARY
or
INTELLIGENCE SUMMARY
(Erase heading not required.)

474TH (SOUTH MIDLAND) FIELD COMPANY, R.E.

Hour, Date, Place	Summary of Events and Information	Remarks and references to Appendices
Feb 1st 1917	Company at HAMEL – No 1 & 2 S/ns cutting trees for Bde – Gen Holland visited for all	
2nd	Coy moved to FROISSY. O.C. returns from G.H.Q.	
3rd	School exams 3 pm	
4th	Co Rested	
5th	No 3 S. to CAPPY to work on D.H.Q. at OLYMPE. Rem and J. Cpl on Truck Board & other furniture & repairs to Camp. French Genie still I/c store to women above at FROISSY WORKSHOPS	
6th – 8th	As above – Picket for S/gd began – various small work. Started up to HERBECOURT Div Dump. 6 Horses I/states to transports range.	
9th	Took over from the French – 7 Nissen huts Completes & two Div HQ.	
10 – 15	Work as above – Baths at ECLUSIER & CAPPY. 5th – Rumour troops about to move again. By splitting Sussex prs & map, inking Irish obstacle, sharpen.	
16th	1 SBC pipe road, Baths & Camp S6 Lynen 14th. In pickets or Baths of Camp S6 Lynen 14th. 3000 pickets cut & sharpened & wiring	

WAR DIARY or INTELLIGENCE SUMMARY

Army Form C. 2118.

(Erase heading not required.)

474TH (SOUTH MIDLAND) FIELD COMPANY R.E.

Hour, Date, Place	Summary of Events and Information	Remarks and references to Appendices
16.2.17	Party 6 split 30/6/12 - work on 14 & 2 Torkon Pumps & men heatings & timbers from A.S.C. huts. Lorry	
16	Wire on A.S.C. Refilling points. FONTAINE le CAPPY	
17	Baths at CAPPY finished. 1100 special pickets for signal	
	made	
18	ECLUSIER Baths finished - sorting of timber completed	
19	At FONSSY	
	hospitals & signals, artillery bridges begun.	
20.21	Battlemore FONSSY finished; INFOUT retrenchant	
	Sir finisher - Start of D.T.C. officers lofven - artillery	
	horse begun - 5th Sussex Company enstrouver	
22	lunt at Leary Camp MERGICOURT running for 3 & 5th	
23	62d Artillery Bridge complete m/g h 2 to no 3 & a.	
	Bath - pump - Lavage or F FONSSY complete - signal public date 340 & 0	Capt Richards returned from leave
24	Artillery Bonar (12) finishes - m/r & 4 sec signal	
25	public complete - 18 men & 5 R.S. Rgt attached (24th)	
	made 200 trench beams 20ft.	
26	Refilling pits of ASC at FONTAINE finished	
	Surface unit 225 trench bonar. In much head as task	
27	admin - return home & 3 P.M. finished	
28	Trench boned track & FONSSY battalion. Baths at Camp 53	J.R. Chapman
	heads complete 300 trench bonar brought	Major

Forms/C. 2118/11.
1:17 W 3299 200,000 (E) 8/14 J.B.C. & A.

CONFIDENTIAL
****

WAR DIARY

of

474th (South Midland) Field Coy. R.E.

WAR DIARY or INTELLIGENCE SUMMARY

Army Form C. 2118.

(Erase heading not required.)

474TH (SOUTH MIDLAND) FIELD COMPANY, R.E.

Hour, Date, Place	Summary of Events and Information	Remarks and references to Appendices
March 1917		
1	The Company at FROISSY with No 3 & 8 at CAPPY. 20 men & Nos 3rd Section attached at PROYART. Work – 4 hand Batt. Sprayers Camp 58, repairs to steam Camp INTERMEDIATE, Carriers for Signal Co'y, Latrines for Camp 47. Bath. FROISSY, Trenchmen (interlacing) – 600' hurdles Roads between CAPPY & ECLUSIER – Pump at various points.	
2	As above – 950' trench mats – latrine frames – welcome & map board for JOPR.	
3	Bath at Camp 58 finished – 790' trench mats – painting frames for G. H.Q.	
4	Bunch & Canal steppes at PROISSY Baths – Lean camp MERICOURT finished – MT Convoits train through fog OZ & MPZ Valley before – 80'0" trench mats – 54 trench ladders.	
5	Service Billy kittens. – moving sheds as above – Boundary heads for Sm mats of Foam – 608' trench heads mats – moving sheds – 200 trench ladders –	
6	Water Connection to OLYMPE finished – 40 Tramway mats mn Latrine for PROISSY Baths.	(DIV. H.Q. = OLYMPE [illegible] 23/3/17)
7	All 5 mechanical pumps running – 180 trench bridge mats Workshop to store lycan – sizes for horses alongside railway at workshop laid. Pads of 24 lorverstine attached from Div. Supp. truly had sundry thaw precaution.	

WAR DIARY
or
INTELLIGENCE SUMMARY

Army Form C. 2118.

474TH (SOUTH MIDLAND) FIELD COMPANY, R.E.

Hour, Date, Place	Summary of Events and Information	Remarks and references to Appendices
March 8 1917	20 tank turfs, 60 tank ladders, 3 trucks & cans sent to for bques & sent up with stores to Div. Dump – 6mm front from Camp 58 – Blast of balls pressed & stn of hires dropped – guns out driven up – painting supply of G. mounts glass frame omitted	
9	No. 1 R.E. employed out on daily report. 100x truck heads 3 men trip truck wars – 12 drivers of ammund charge pump at grazing Stu repairs & tank mounters. 5 sheers withdrawn.	
10	Carriers of signals 80% finished – repairs to preservatory – from f Camp 58 finished. 6 camp trucks made (6cms). 6 gun butt train finished. 180x head boards worn – repairs to R.E. hut. Bris frame (box) in Reinforcement Camp (52) – repairs to Camp 47. 2/Lt Sinclair taken over a sec road rung arts – Sinclair (Cpl).	2nd Lt Sinclair returns from course at Div. Schl.
11	at 6 pm – may fires – testing streams in tartle wagon.	
12	General work in stores. Carriers for signals finished. Tee made for training wire (c. 145 Inf. Bde.) & charge of guncotton made up for demolishing enemy dug-outs &fc for 477 Fd Co.	It to cavalier passed to Majr H. Chisolm at attch to GLRE. Div HQ. (until of…)
13	General work as above. Water troughs for D.A.C. N.C.O's School Campton.	

Army Form C. 2118.

WAR DIARY
or
INTELLIGENCE SUMMARY
(Erase heading not required.)

474TH (SOUTH MIDLAND) FIELD COMPANY, R.E.

No. ....
Date ....

Hour, Date, Place	Summary of Events and Information	Remarks and references to Appendices
March 14th 1917.	General work in Store; Watering Place for D.A.C. on CAPPY-FRISE Road. Well at 3rd Fd Ambulance repaired. Boot washing hut at Camp 56. Instructions received to move Bridging equipment to FRISE by 17th.	
15th	General work in Store; Watering Place for D.A.C. Rush for Reinforcement Camp MERIGNOLLES. Orders received at 11.40 p.m. to move Bridging Pontoons to FRISE immediately.	
16th	General Work in Store: Orders received at 11.0 p.m. to move with 3 Sections to FRISE at 5.0 a.m. 17/3/17 by motor lorry for Bridging operations to relieve 475 Coy R.E.	16th The following were presented with their ribbons of their medals by the Corps Commander. C.S.M. Denham DCM & Medaile Militaire L/Cpl. Edmunds D.C.M. Sgt. Baldwin M.M. Corp. Mitchell C. M.M. " Cpl Lostryan M.M. C.Q.M.S Williams M.S.M.
17th	3 Sections moved at 5.20 a.m. by lorry leaving No 2 Section to transport at FROISY. 2nd/Lt. Wilson remained in charge of Store. No 1 & 4 Sections ferried 2 Coys 8th R. Warwick Regt. over SOMME to HALLE during night. No. 3 Section continued work on Bridge over Canal at BAZINCOURT FARM. Bridge over Canal begun by 475 Fd G. R.E. at BAZINCOURT FARM. No 2 Section moved from FROISY to FRISE.	
18th	Coy housed in huts ½ mile to BIACHES & Horse on foot to FAUBOURG de PARIS for Bridging operations in PERONNE. 5 Pontoons off lorries from Pontoon Park at BIACHE & rowed up Canal to PERONNE buttresses. 3 Bridges [H. horse transport erected: (2) 1 Pontoon Bridge over Canal with (2nd Hunting.) Bridge on trestles built in SOMME and (3) Bridge on trestles built in lift of existing pile. over SOMME. 200 Inf. 8.30 a.c. 7.0 p.m. in relief.	C.S.M Denham to England. (2) 2/Lt C. Cooper (3) Lt. G. Hunter
19th	(2) 8 1 Trestle Bridges (2nd Lt. Grisham)	

Army Form C. 2118.

WAR DIARY
or
INTELLIGENCE SUMMARY
(Erase heading not required.)

Instructions regarding War Diaries and Intelligence Summaries are contained in F. S. Regs, Part II. and the Staff Manual respectively. Title pages will be prepared in manuscript.

474TH (SOUTH MIDLAND) FIELD COMPANY, R.E.

Date.................

Hour, Date, Place	Summary of Events and Information	Remarks and references to Appendices
March 20th 1917	Bridging Continued. 5.0 a.m. to 7.0 p.m. Orders received at 5.0 p.m.	
21st	to make bridges capable of carrying commercial lorries. 2 Rollafoot 200 Infantry to assist in assembling & clearing streets. Pontoon Bridge for horse transport over Canal Completed.	
	Heavy bridge over Canal started. Coy Transport moved from FROISY to LA CHAPELETTE. La MIRE Bridge taken over from 477 Coy R.E. "17th Dublin Fus."	
22nd 23rd	Bridging Continued: Heavy trestle Bridge over Canal abandoned in adjunct of working at bottom of Canal. Heavy Pontoon Bridge over Canal built with Rails & in place of baulks. Wooden trestles at shores the other line	1. 2/Lt Wilson reported at Coy fm FROISY. 2. 2/Lt Dublin Fus."
24th	Bridges completed all open for traffic at 10.30 p.m.	2. 2/Lt Browne & 2/Lt Wilson in charge.
	Maintenance of Bridge, double decking – bracing etc. Approaches. Clearing sheds etc. Footbridge started to N side of main bridge	in gin Chevrolet's design.
25th	do. for 24th	
26th	do. for 25th. Traverson of an Welden Trestle broke under 60 pounder gun. at 8.15 p.m. New Traverson strengthend with "U" Iron Bands placed in position by 1.15 a.m. & bridge reopened for traffic.	
27th	Reconnoitered line of Resistance from MAR QUAIX to LIERAMONT with G.S.O.1.	
28th	Coy moved hd N°3 Section Transport to Bois de BUIRE with Biorracs. Wells in TEMPLEUX HONGAVENES Reconn'd.	
	N° 3 Section maintaining Bridges in PERONNE.	

Army Form C. 2118.

474TH (SOUTH MIDLAND) FIELD COMPANY, R.E.

WAR DIARY
INTELLIGENCE SUMMARY

(Erase heading not required.)

Place	Date	Hour	Summary of Events and Information	Remarks and references to Appendices
	March 29th		Work on Wells in Templeux Largeuenes started. Well in SAULCOURT reconnoitered. trys to in Cruciform forts sited with B.M. 143 Inf Bde. VILLERS FAUCON reconnoitered for Punch Batt.	
	30th		Work on Wells in TEMPLEUX, LONGAVESNES, & RIEN COURT Cruciform forts taped out + dug. 2nd Lt Jim Wilson & 2nd Lt G.J. Cooper i/c 143 Bde section. 2nd Lt Churchn & 2nd Lt A.J. Skinner i/c 145 Bde section. No 3 Subsection joined Coy.	
	31		No 2 + No 4 Sections moved to TEMPEUX Querreu (bivouac) Transport joined Coy. No 3 Section taking down old German wire near MARQUAIX + getting ready for use a line of Resistance for 145 Bde. 143 Inf Bde wiring with scount wire pickets mins hinges up from PERONNE.	

[signature]
474 Co R.E.

CONFIDENTIAL.

War Diary

of

474th (S.M.) Field Coy R.E.

From 1st April 1917 to 30th April 1917.

WAR DIARY or INTELLIGENCE SUMMARY

Army Form C. 2118

674TH
(SOUTH MIDLAND)
FIELD COMPANY, R.E.

Date		Summary of Events and Information	Remarks and references to Appendices
April 1st 1917		Work on Wells in TEMPLEUX, LONGAVESNES & DRIENCOURT continued. Erection from Posts in line of Resistance dug & wiring commenced. Line runs from SERAMONT in front of LONGAVESNES to MARQUAIX	
2nd		No 1 Section with 200 Inf cleaning streets in ROISEL employing civilian unused erratic No 3 Section dismantling German hut nets for erection by 145 Inf Bde Section 2 & 4 working on wells in TEMPLEUX & LONGAVESNES. Wells obtained 1 Wirest fixed in TEMPLEUX	
3rd		Section 1 & 3 H.Q. moved to BOIS de TINCOURT T6d85. (Sht 62c NE) Work on wells in TEMPLEUX & LONGAVESNES continued. German line dismantled near MARQUAIX HAMEL. Road Crater at K10d made passable for horse transport.	
4th		Road deviations round craters at E30c09, JE18d30, & E8657 made passable for horse traffic. Work on Wells continued	
5th		Road deviation in above made passable for both lorries. Work on Wells continued. Bolt wall revising grid installed at deviation in TEMPLEUX. Retimbering of top of LONGAVESNES well requised. Road deviation at K17A started by Section No 3.	
6th		Water carts being filled at TEMPLEUX. Work on Wells in LONGAVESNES continued	
7th		Road deviation for field lorries round crater at K17A completed. Arrangements for house watering at TEMPLEUX started. Retiming of large well at LONGAVESNES completed. Site for Adrian huts reconnoitred in ST EMILIE VILLERS FAUCON.	
8th		Water supply at TEMPLEUX & LONGAVESNES. Roofs of Batt. H.Q. at EPEHY being strengthened with sleepers & bricks no heating engine. Camouflage Posts in Green line sited. Site for Adrian huts (pepers) in VILLERS FAUCON.	
9th		Work continued on cellars of Batt. H.Q. at EPEHY. & on Wells supply to TEMPLEUX & LONGAVESNES in VILLERS FAUCON	
10th		Camouflage of posts in picture in Railway Cutting VILLERS FAUCON.	

WAR DIARY
or
INTELLIGENCE SUMMARY.
(Erase heading not required.)

Army Form C. 2118.

47TH (SOUTH MIDLAND) FIELD COMPANY, R.E.

Place	Date	Hour	Summary of Events and Information	Remarks and references to Appendices
April	11th		2 Sections H.Q moved to Railway cutting near VILLERS FAUCON (sheet 62c NE. E 23 d 52)	
	12th		Work on Water supply TEMPLEUX. LONGAVESNES. Continued, also strengthening of Batt H.Q. in EPEHY. Wiring party on Brown Line arrange with 125 Inf Bde but did not materialize. Water Supply TEMPLEUX LONGAVESNE ST EMILIE Batt H.Q in EPEHY. Sappers worked on Brown Line	Major McClean returned to Corps CRES office
	13th		+C.R.E. visited some of the posts. Wiring on Brown Line with 125 Inf Bde. (7 hours 5 mins) Work on Brown Support line with 100 Inf. Digging cruciform posts. Water supply as above +Batt H.Q. Artillery O.P. reconnoitered.	
	14		Laying Brown Line & Brown Support. Clearing site of water trough for Ste EMILIE. Transport trough TEMPLEUX strong trenches. Bringing up EVILLERS FAUCON STN trolls tracks supply EPEHY continued.	
	15/16		Lorries about — work & Cullan EPEHY continued.	
	17		No 2 Sn. Came up EVILLERS FAUCON	
	18		3 Ofr & 74 men Saw East EPEHY — Adrian huts begun at Ste EMILIE	
	19		remainder of 1 & 3 Sn to OC EPEHY. No 2 Sn worked on Div H.Q.	
	20		No 2 Sn in Brown Route Ste EMILIE. Nos 1 & 3 on Brown & Brown support lines	2nd Lt Penman went on leave
	21		No 4 Sn moved from TEMPLEUX to VILLERS FAUCON. 2 Adrian huts completed	
	23		Capt Richards joined by C.E. to take over New Blue Line	
	24		Work on Pt Aerien Huts water point Ste EMILIE (Horses 40?) complete. One of on New Blue Line.	
	26-27		Work on above	
	28		No 4 St- EPEHY – work on Green Line begun	2nd Lt Sinclair from 1/3rd Inf Bde
	29 30		Work on infantry on Green (New Blue) line, work on Brown line continued	

O.C. 474th (S.M.) FIELD COY. R.E.(T).

J Stewart
MAJOR.

Vol 29

CONFIDENTIAL.
****

WAR   DIARY

of

474th (South Midland) Field Company R.E.

From 1st. May 1917......to......31st May 1917.

Army Form C. 2118.

WAR DIARY
or
INTELLIGENCE SUMMARY.
(Erase heading not required.)

Instructions regarding War Diaries and Intelligence Summaries are contained in F. S. Regs., Part II. and the Staff Manual respectively. Title pages will be prepared in manuscript.

474TH (SOUTH MIDLAND) FIELD CO. PANY., R.E.

Place	Date	Hour	Summary of Events and Information	Remarks and references to Appendices
EPEHY	May 1917		Company less 1st & 4th Septs at EPEHY. 1st & 4th Septs under Capt Richards at VILLERS FAUCON. All sections working on Green Line - night work - making & constructn of strong points, localities, wire & M.G. posts	Lieut Spencer reported from leave.
	2		As above	
	3		Company attached to 42nd Divn	
	4-6		Work on Green Line continued	
	7		New Bn HQ at Ft Central S.W. of PETIT PRIEL Farm opened 10 am	
	8-10		2nd entanguimts on Ls 3 Sns No 2&5. Preparing frames etc. - counterplots. 24 hours' shifts. Infantry parties on Green Line Supply construction, trenches and communication trenches.	
	11		Work stopped at 10 am. Frames were placed at 2'8" centres intervals 6 mins intervals between mines (extra later). Frames 5' x 3' stakes in places & slope 1'/1' 6'. Stirring. Apt 3½ mins and it was – 9 gallows with upright 7' frames & posts, 6 horz & sloping frames and 3 hurdles staked simultaneously with 7 staples all work hours incl to 429 F.C.	
	12		Co moved to PERONNE	
	13		Lodging Poitou Surgical - ??? return ???	
	14		Repairs 4 7mm Howr. Rly. & wing & 7mm wagons - working at R.E. Stores - Sn.	

Army Form C. 2118.

WAR DIARY
or
INTELLIGENCE SUMMARY.
(Erase heading not required.)

Instructions regarding War Diaries and Intelligence Summaries are contained in F.S. Regs., Part II. and the Staff Manual respectively. Title pages will be prepared in manuscript.

474TH (SOUTH MIDLAND) FIELD COMPANY, R.E.

Place	Date	Hour	Summary of Events and Information	Remarks and references to Appendices
	15 Aug		Coy moved to COMBLES - advance party with lorry from pioneers to Camp	
	16		Coy moved to Camp at S7C - I.47.c.19	
	17		Coy moved to LEBUCQUIÈRES - work in BEAUMETZ - MORCHIES line begun	
			with 200 inf by night 200 by day, 3 sec sappers lorrying (tested) & sapper	2/Lt Browne went on leave
	18		work continues as above	
	19		As above - new section in D142	
	20		Took over work in Baths VELU, starts baths HAPLINCOURT- Hands over BEAUMETZ	
			MORCHIES line to 5 R.E. Pioneers. Took over Bng at work in left Bde Area	
	21		Baths continues - took over Coroot Stores - Inf cut 2½ section	
	22		As above - work also in Canal drain + tunnels HERMIES [green turnips	
	23		As above - no party by day. Sapper WITCOMB P.E. contrabalutes to dinner ?	
	24		As above - 1 NCO with 12 infy by day.	Major H Christie went on leave
	25		as above	
	26		as above	
	27		as above	
	28		as above - Well at HERMIES cleared to depth of 103ft.- Baths at FREMICOURT started	2/Lt C.E. Shrilcay rejoined Coy from Class D in R.E.
	29		as above	
	30		as above	
	31		as above - HAPLINCOURT & VELU Baths finished. FREMICOURT & Hutch Bath finished. Walls	2/Lt Brown returned from leave
			& ring facing well to 60. Well HERMIES cleared to depth of 113ft.	Richard P Capt.

A 8534 Wt. W4973/M687 750,000 8/16 D D & L Ltd. Forms/C2118/11

War Diary

of 474th (S. Mid) Field Coy. R.E.

for month of June 1917

Volume 30.

WAR DIARY
or
INTELLIGENCE SUMMARY.
(Erase heading not required.)

Army Form C. 2118.

474TH (SOUTH MIDLAND) FIELD COMPANY, R.E.

Place	Date	Hour	Summary of Events and Information	Remarks and references to Appendices
	June 1st 1917.		Dugout work in Left Bde area continued. Gas check probes fitted to Dugouts in Left Bde area. Well at HERMIES cleaned to depth of 116 ft. Work stopped on FREMICOURT Butts.	2/Lt C.W. Walton went on leave 6th inst.
	2-5		As above.	
	6		As above. Materials for Butts moved from FREMICOURT to BEUGNY. & erection started.	
	7		As above.	
	8		As above. Plunge Bath started at HAPLINCOURT. 15 old concrete cistern cleaned. Walls to be slaged daily as a sewage sump for drainage made.	Major H. Chinoll returned from leave. 2nd Lt J.E.W. Brown went to IV Corps School (Onl)
	9		As above.	
	10		As above. Screening road from VELU to HERMIES.	
	11-12		Work on dugouts started in Right Bde area.	
	13		Div. R.E. Sports. Work on Dugouts continued.	
	14		Work on Dugouts continued, also work on Butts, BEUGNY & HAPLINCOURT. Well at HERMIES 145 ft deep & Water coming (?) in.	2nd Lt J.E.W. Walton returned from leave.
	15		As above. Dugout work finished in Left Bde area with 1 exception in Left Bn.	
	16		As above. HAPLINCOURT Plunge Bath finished. Work on BEAUMETZ - MORCHIES line taken over from 5th Sussex.	Major H. Chinoll went to CRE's office. 2nd/Lt Sim Walton went to ?
	17-19		As above.	
	20		As above: Lectures of C.R.E. on Elementary Principles of wiring at BAPAUME on 20/6/17	

Army Form C. 2118.

WAR DIARY
or
INTELLIGENCE SUMMARY.
(Erase heading not required.)

474TH
(SOUTH MIDLAND)
FIELD COMPANY, R.E.

Place	Date	Hour	Summary of Events and Information	Remarks and references to Appendices
June 21st	1917			
	27th		BEAUMETZ - MORCHIES Line work continued with 2 companies of infantry. Wiring completion - Defensive + Tactical - digging of pits & marking out posts + C.T.s continued. HAPLINCOURT Pump task completed - Drainage shed & steps made. - BEUGNY Baths complete. Spring in canal at J34 d.75 (Sheet 57c) protected, tank finished. 12 Bangalore Torpedoes made. Frameworks erected for Baths, Haynichs in 143 Bde area, + for D.A.C. Work on dugouts continued. 'Section in Left Bde area - 1 section in Right Bde area. 1 mobile 'oddjobs', well at FREMICOURT. Well raisers. Relining well at FREMICOURT. 400 gallon tanks erected along 60 cm track near BEUGNY, BEAUMETZ, VELU & April heap in J34 d.	2nd Lt Activity rejoined Coy from 5th F.S.C. on 26/6/17
	28		Water raisers at HERMIES with drawer from store. Relining well at FREMICOURT finished.	2nd Lt Wilson returned from leave
	29th		Work stopped on all dugouts + on BEAUMETZ - MORCHIES Line. Vehicles packed. Major N. Chinnock returned Coy from CRE's Office. 2nd Lts E.C. Light (temp) attached Company to 4796 & 4795 3rd F.A. Co. Sundon	475

A5834 Wt. W4973/M687 750,000 8/16 D. D. & L. Ltd. Forms/C.2118/13.

Army Form C. 2118.

WAR DIARY
or
INTELLIGENCE SUMMARY.
(Erase heading not required.)

Instructions regarding War Diaries and Intelligence Summaries are contained in F. S. Regs., Part II. and the Staff Manual respectively. Title pages will be prepared in manuscript.

Place	Date	Hour	Summary of Events and Information	Remarks and references to Appendices
	30		Company moved to GOMIECOURT. Two offrs left behind to hand over to relieving coy on the 3rd July.	A Church map 4/4 POY R.E.

[Stamp: 474TH (SOUTH MIDLAND) FIELD COMPANY, R.E.]

War Diary (A.F.C.2118)
of 474th (S.Mid.) Field Coy R.E.
for month of July 1917
Volume No

474TH
(SOUTH MIDLAND)
FIELD COMPANY, R.E.
No. 31/7/17

C.J. Godfrey, Major,
O.C. 474th S.M. Field Coy. R.E.(T)

WAR DIARY or INTELLIGENCE SUMMARY

Army Form C. 2118.

474TH (SOUTH MIDLAND) FIELD COMPANY, R.E.

Place	Date	Hour	Summary of Events and Information	Remarks and references to Appendices
July 1917	1-4		Company at GOMAIECOURT. Programme of Training - musketry, bomb throwing - revising heavy gun - subjects - explaining with football periods. In afternoon and Physical Drill (when fine) from 6.30 - 7 am was carried out	
	5		Company moved to POPERINGHE STN (near POPERINGHE) by train. Transport of the Coy, half 475 + AV Cable Sec were sent in advance by march of pioneers. This took nearly 4 hours. Train starts 4 pm	
	6		Arrive POPERINGHE 5 am - Breakfasts - marches to wood Anims 10 am Bivouacked. 2000 x N.º 1 BRANDHOEK annex Camouflage tarpaulin fixed. Dragoon CHIDDY wounded + D Rider Landon killed. bombed at night . round 1000 x S.W.	
	7		Moved to L Camp near WATOU. Rested.	
	8			
	11		Camp orders No 39 Para. Secs 2,3,4 with two of the moves to Camp North Sheet 28 I & G 92	

Army Form C. 2118.

WAR DIARY
or
INTELLIGENCE SUMMARY.
(Erase heading not required.)

Instructions regarding War Diaries and Intelligence Summaries are contained in F.S. Regs., Part II. and the Staff Manual respectively. Title pages will be prepared in manuscript.

474TH (SOUTH MIDLAND) FIELD COMPANY, R.E.

Place	Date	Hour	Summary of Events and Information	Remarks and references to Appendices
July	12 & 13	1917	Work on Dug-outs near bridge 1A, and in artillery siding at ENGLISH FARM continued	Sgt. GOOD wounded
	14		As above. Heavy shelling (including gas) and capture of neighbouring Gun Group/s	
	15		Dug-outs as above — Stop work to dig-out near Bridge 2A	2nd Lt. HUNTER killed.
	16		No 1 Sec. replaced No 3 Sec — Work much delayed by shelling	
	17		First gun emplacement Iredale, from the 2nd heavy howitzers in dug-out last night	5 O.R. wounded (incl. Bates)
	18		ENGLISH Farm Track complete	2nd Lt. Sec Browne returned from camp / hosp.
	19		No 3 Sec. with 2 Lt. Skinner detailed to help XVIII Corps Exploit in Chinese attack. Sec moved to JAN DER BIEZEN. Artillery Bridge at C21 c & 9 erected on rafts	2 OR wounded
	20,21		Work as above — gun down fitter to own dug-out.	
	22		No 2 Sec returned to POEZELHOEK, leaving only 2 Secs & Canal Banks 13 men & no 2 gassed	2 OR wounded
	23, 20th			
	24		3 weeks in Dug-outs, move improvements for arty.	
	25		No 3 & 4 Sec returned to PEZELHOEK. Early Coy came out of 48 Div.	
	26		Work in Camp — installation maunde. Repairing bridges. attempts laubre arms canal	
	27		Start of late work stopped by Summer School. Casualties from Jan: 17-2; 18-2; 19-3; 20-1; 22-1; 23-3; 24-3; 25-3; 26-2.	
	28		Gas Helmet Drill — whole dirt & camp	
	29		Reinforcement of 48 arrived	
	30		Church Parade / afternoon I.	
	31		Trek to Sec (also a few parties) marches to camp near VLAMERTINGHE at 3 pm. Work on BATH ROAD from HAMMOND'S CORNER to ADMIRAL'S ROAD	Sec PTE wounded

J. C. Annand

WA 32

War Diary (AF C2118)

of 474th (S. Midland.) Field Company R.E. (T.F.)

for Month of August 1917

Volume 32.

474TH
(SOUTH MIDLAND)
FIELD COMPANY, R.E.
No.
Date.

WAR DIARY or INTELLIGENCE SUMMARY

Army Form C. 2118.

474th (SOUTH MIDLAND) FIELD COMPANY, R.E.

Place	Date	Hour	Summary of Events and Information	Remarks and references to Appendices
August 1917	1st		4 Sections worked on Batt. Rd. Track in C.21.d. near HILLTOP FARM. (Map Ref: Sheet 28 NW.2 1:10000)	
	2		No 4 Section on Batt Rd. Track: 1, 2 + 3 Sections on Trench board track from Buff Rd. C.21.d.15 to ADMIRAL'S Rd. C.22.a.23.	
	3rd		4 Sections on Trench board track. 2nd Lt. Curnston attached to 104th Lab. Cy R.E. till afternoon of 6th Aug.	
	4		ditto. 2 Sections resting.	
	5		O.C. + 4 Section moved to Canal Bank + took over charge from 225th Fld Cy R.E. Work recommenced 1, 3, 4 Sections T.B. track to ALBERTA. No 2 Section in billets. 48th Div. Relieved 39th Div. on night 5/6th	
	6		No 2 section in billets. night 6/7. 3 + 4 sections finished Trench board track to ALBERTA.	
	7		No 3 Section reconnoitred Artillery track from Admirals Rd to RACE COURSE FARM 1,2,4 French board track to JULIET FARM.	
	8		No 3 Section on Artillery track as above. 2 Sections T.B. track to JULIET Farm.	
	9		2nd Lt. D M Wilson + 9 O.Rs attached to 145 Inf. Bde. till Aug. 16th (2 days) for training with Bde. for laying "jumping off" tapes in 2 days. Section on T.B. track + Art. tracks.	
	10		night 9/10. Pack section started carrying materials forward to CORNER COT. 2/Lt. J. Cooper moved from horse lines at PEREL HOEK to Canal bank Pack Cy (No4) R.E. moved to DAM BRE Camp. 474 Section with 29 animals. m having been killed on night 9/10.	
			Sections worked on T.B. + Art. tracks.	

Army Form C. 2118.

WAR DIARY
or
INTELLIGENCE SUMMARY.
(Erase heading not required.)

Instructions regarding War Diaries and Intelligence Summaries are contained in F.S. Regs., Part II. and the Staff Manual respectively. Title pages will be prepared in manuscript.

[Stamp: 474TH (SOUTH MIDLAND) FIELD COMPANY, R.E.]

Place	Date	Hour	Summary of Events and Information	Remarks and references to Appendices
August	11	1917	Sections working on Tracks (trench board & artillery). Ref. map 28 N.W.2. 1:10,000	
	12		Posts within working at light-alleys from ADMIRALS Rd Dump to KITCHENERS WOOD.	
	13		ditto	
	14		ditto 1½ Sections assisting 477 Fd Coy on trench board track from Wilson Farm to Boundary Rd.	
	15		ditto	
	16		Attack by 145 Inf Bde. 2nd Lt E M Wilson returned to Coy after being to enquiry off Aljaks 2nd Lt C W Watson detailed to investigate water supply for men who were able to forward 2nd Lt E M Browne on in (failure of attack). 2 Sections on Rd from VANHEULE Farm to St Julien. ST. JULIEN.	
	17		Stood by	
	18		2 Sections & 2 Platoons R. Sussex on Trench board track from ALBERTA & STEENBEEK. 1 Section repairing trench board tracks. 1 Section assisting by Pack animals (11) returned to PESELHOEK Tram port cant. with 2nd Lt C J Cooper	
	19		No 4 Section O.C. moved to HAMPSHIRE Farm & camped in trenches there. No 3 – Consolidated HILLOCH Farm 19/20. (C.12a 65) No 2 – Trench board tracks.	
	20		No 1 stood by. No 2 moved to HAMPSHIRE Farm. – 294 [struck through] No 1 moved to HAMPSHIRE Farm	
	–		No 1, 3 & ½ 2 Shelters at HAMPSHIRE Farm. No 4 resting during day. UWright cleared trees on St Julien –	
	21.			

WAR DIARY
INTELLIGENCE SUMMARY
(Erase heading not required.)

Army Form C. 2118.

474TH (SOUTH MIDLAND) FIELD COMPANY, R.E.

Place	Date	Hour	Summary of Events and Information	Remarks and references to Appendices
	August 22nd 1917		No 1 & 3 stood by. No 4 shelter at HAMPSHIRE Farm. No 2 trench board track 2nd Lt A.J. Skinner gassed by shell gas & left unit.	
	23rd		2nd Lt C.J. Cooper moved up to HAMPSHIRE Farm took over No 2 shelter which working a night of 23/24 on shelter East of St Julien, returning on night 24/25. Trench board tracks maintained near HAMPSHIRE Farm.	
	24th		Shelters & shelters continued near HAMPSHIRE Farm. Trench board tracks maintained.	
	25.		1 & 3 Sections worked on making camouflage for 143 Inf Bde. with 40 8th R War R + 1 Pl. R Sussex. No 4 on trench board track repairs. Major Helliwell wounded slightly & admitted to 61 C.C.S. 2nd Lt B.M. Wilson went to XVIII Corps Inf. School.	
	26		Sections 1, 3, & 4 day on shelters at HAMPSHIRE Farm. No 4 section reporo. French (m.s) night 26/27 No 2 Section arriving inf (143 Bde) with camouflage. Capt Starland moved with orderly room to Canal bank. No progress with camouflage owing to non arrival of Transport - In shelling material got up to VAN HEULE Fm at 2.30 am 27/8/17 - several horses killed	

Army Form C. 2118.

WAR DIARY
or
INTELLIGENCE SUMMARY.
(Erase heading not required.)

Instructions regarding War Diaries and Intelligence Summaries are contained in F. S. Regs., Part II. and the Staff Manual respectively. Title pages will be prepared in manuscript.

[Stamp: 47th SOUTH MIDLAND FIELD COMPANY, R.E.]

Place	Date	Hour	Summary of Events and Information	Remarks and references to Appendices
August	27		Work on shelters continued. No 2 Sn. hrs 3 & 4 Sn. started night clearing road to SULLEN L.TRIANGLE Fm. & attempts to wire Gun pits in front of MILLOCK Fm.	
	28		No work	
	29		Cy moved to PESELHOEK — O.C. reproves by Infantry Bde — Martin "Explosives of all Sorts" 1st Sy time attempting — No 3 Sn. made "Tovey" traths" — remainder Muskitz. Afternoon 17-31/8/17	Capt Pickerks 2/Lt Cowper instr Team
	30			
	31		No parties out 12-20 Sappers were employed a various work at PETER HOEK. Duty which formed them by was at time List of Casualties of Events is attached	

[Signature] N. Chiesa
MAJOR,
O.C. 47 S.M. FIELD COY. R.E.(T).

attached to War Diary for August 1917

CASUALTIES. - AUGUST, 1917.

474th (South Midland) Field Company, R.E.

Date	Reg. No.	Rank	Name		Remarks
5.8.17	494474	Sergt.	Gardiner,	A.	Wounded - Rejoined 10/9/17
8.8.17	494941	Sapper	Marsh,	C.E.	Wounded
10.8.17	494404	Driver	Lawrence,	F.C.	Killed - Buried: 10/8/17
10.8.17	494803	Driver	Alford,	W.E.	Wounded
10.8.17	494176	Sergt.	Dunk,	J.	Wounded
10.8.17	170657	Sapper	Williams,	G.H.	Wounded
10.8.17	494785	Sapper	Wiltshire,	A.G.	Wounded
11.8.17	495003	Sapper	Cox,	A.J.L.	Wounded
11.8.17	404268	Sapper	Simpson,	A.B.	Wounded
11.8.17	446929	Sapper	Barton,	A.	Wounded
12.8.17	494034	Driver	Milton,	G.H.	Wounded
12.8.17	412064	Sapper	Gardner,	A.	Wounded - At Duty
13.8.17	193615	Sapper	Luty,	H.	Wounded
14.8.17	495106	Sapper	Perry,	H.J.	Wounded
14.8.17	426552	Sapper	Pierpoint,	W.	Gassed
15.8.17	176700	Sapper	Warrell,	C.W.	Wounded
15.8.17	212546	Sapper	Yates,	J.	Wounded
16.8.17	494090	II. Corpl.	Edmonds,	A.E.	Killed - Buried: 18/8/17
16.8.17	494761	Sapper	Goodlife,	J.	Wounded
16.8.17	404305	Sapper	Fyfe,	W.C.	Wounded
16.8.17	498401	Sapper	Brookman,	J.J.	Wounded
16.8.17	420459	Sapper	Rowland,	J.	Wounded
16.8.17	188506	Sapper	Money,	A.	Wounded
16.8.17	494154	Lce.Cpl.	Bowers,	W.S.	Wounded
16.8.17	422530	Sapper	Magee,	J.L.	Wounded
16.8.17	494677	Sapper	Moore,	J.	Wounded
16.8.17	548112	Sapper	Bodger,	E.	Wounded
17.8.17	494243	Sapper	Coles,	A.	Wounded - At Duty
21.8.17	554407	Sapper	Bent,	J.W.	Killed
21.8.17	551154	Sapper	Dore,	R.	Killed — Buried: 21.8.17
21.8.17	494539	Sapper	Parsons,	S.C.	Killed
21.8.17	477022	Sapper	Relph,	P.	Killed

21. 8. 17	486187	Sapper	Toft,	G.	Wounded
21. 8. 17	476345	Sapper	Asling,	J. A.	Wounded
21. 8. 17	495046	Sapper	Mountain,	A.	Wounded Rejd 29/8/17
21. 8. 17	524401	Sapper	Brockett,	W. J.	Wounded
21. 8. 17	526234	Sapper	Gardner,	W. J.	Wounded - At Duty.
23. 8. 17	494112	Corpl.	Harding,	A.	Wounded
23. 8. 17	446981	Sapper	Jones,	J. H.	Wounded
23. 8. 17	494899	Lce. Corpl.	Cocks,	A.	Wounded
24. 8. 17	496751	Sapper	Townsend,	W.R.D.	Killed. - Buried: 24/8/17
24. 8. 17	216580	Sapper	Baxter,	W.S.	Wounded
24. 8. 17	216427	Sapper	Bellaby,	C.	Wounded - (outwardly) Severe Shock
25. 8. 17	494098	Sapper	Williams,	A. A.	Wounded
		MAJOR	H. CLISSOLD.		Wounded. Rejd 28/8/17
25. 8. 17	404301	Sapper	Cathro,	W.	Wounded
25. 8. 17	495161	Sapper	Woodley,	H. J.	Wounded
25. 8. 17	404324	Sapper	Miller,	W.S.	Wounded.

474TH
(SOUTH MIDLAND)
FIELD COMPANY, R.E.

No.
Date.

Vol 33

War Diary

of 474th (S. Mid) Field Coy R.E. (T.F.)

September 1917

Volume 33.

Army Form C. 2118.

WAR DIARY
or
INTELLIGENCE SUMMARY.
(Erase heading not required.)

Instructions regarding War Diaries and Intelligence Summaries are contained in F. S. Regs., Part II. and the Staff Manual respectively. Title pages will be prepared in manuscript.

474TH (SOUTH MIDLAND) FIELD COMPANY, R.E.

Place	Date	Hour	Summary of Events and Information	Remarks and references to Appendices
RESEL HOEK	Sep/17		Company attended Baths at POPERINGHE	
	2 (Sun)		Church Parade	
	3		No 3 Sn R.A. Camp repairs Fig cleated, nos 1 & 2 musketry (rifle range) trench about Camp. No 4 Tents & Trestles at XVIII Corps Group — Drill for all	
	4		Nos 1 & 2 Trench of Truth, 3 Wiring Carts, 4 wiring & musketry & grenades & Drill for all no 1 Bomb Cart, 2 setting wiring & repairs, 3 RA Camp & wiring & Test of Trestle	
	5		heavicup, 1 work all camp 2 working carts musketry (rifle range) 3 RA Camp & muskets	
	6		(rifle range) 4 Trestle Test — Battle Starts in Camp.	
	7		1 & 2 work in Camp, 3 RA Camp trench in our Camp, 4 Trestle Test.	
	8		12 St work in Camp 4 Trestle Test, 3 work & Camp & RA Camp	
	9 (Sun)		Drill 10 a.m. Church Parade 3 pm	
	10		Gas meeting NISSEN HUTS AT SIEGE JUNCTION are working 5 Camps	Lt Cooper returned from leave
	11		3	1 musketry on 40" range	
	12		3	9 do	
	13		2	2 in Camp	
				1 musketry	
	14		4	do	Capt Richards returned from leave.
	15		2	2 gun duty	
	16		3	1 do	
	17		3	1 in camp	Major Edwards & 2 N/COs went to ?
	18		3	1 — 2 livens musketry do	ZUTKERQUE for RE Training with the Div.
				1 — Alisons musketry do	

Army Form C. 2118.

WAR DIARY
or
INTELLIGENCE SUMMARY.
(Erase heading not required.)

474TH (SOUTH MIDLAND) FIELD COMPANY, R.E.

Place	Date	Hour	Summary of Events and Information	Remarks and references to Appendices
PESELHOEK	Sept 1917.			
	19		Shooting completion on 40ᵗʰ Range – rest of day on holiday.	
	20		3 Sections erecting NISSEN Huts at Siege Camp. – 1 Section experimenting with Welden trestle with transport of R.S. Joists & white pine.	
	21		Major Chisold came back from Divr. for afternoon & returned in morning of 22ⁿᵈ. 3 Section erecting NISSEN Huts at Liege Camp. 1 Section with Welden Trestle	
	22		do	
	23		do	in Camp. Staff report 2nd Member injured
	24		do	from 2nd Canadian Inf. Corps
	25		do	
	26		at Hospital Farm	
	27		Head Quarters and Sappers moved to Canal Bank to relieve 503 Ind Cy R.E. of 53ʳᵈ Divn. Transport moved to Marsh Farm. (H3.c.) sheet 28 N.W.	began closely to the 65 reformed Coy.
	28		Work on Shelters behind CALIFORNIA TRENCH. – enemy shelling. also Capt W.J. Butt & 2/Lieut Barker, Baker, Allen & 13 wounded.	Major H. Chisold Killed by 6
	29		Work on Shelters behind California Trench continued & repairs to dugouts in Canal bank	
	30		ditto	

K.E. Richard Cliffe
O.C. 474ᵗʰ (S.M.) FIELD COY. R.E. (T.)

Vol 34

War Diary
of

474th (S. MID.) FIELD COY., R.E.

for month of October 1917

Volume 34

474TH
(SOUTH MIDLAND)
FIELD COMPANY, R.E.
No........
Date........

Army Form C. 2118.

474TH.
(SOUTH MIDLAND)
FIELD COMPANY, R.E.
No...................
Date.................

WAR DIARY
or
INTELLIGENCE SUMMARY.
(Erase heading not required.)

Instructions regarding War Diaries and Intelligence
Summaries are contained in F. S. Regs., Part II.
and the Staff Manual respectively. Title pages
will be prepared in manuscript.

Place	Date	Hour	Summary of Events and Information	Remarks and references to Appendices
October 1917	1st		H.Q. and Sappers at CANAL Bank: Horse Lines at (H 36) MARSH Farm sheet 28 N.W. 3 sections working on shelters in Old German Front Line (CALIFORNIA). 1 section repairing dugouts in CANAL BANK.	
	2nd		3 sections on shelters in CALIFORNIA. 1 section on accommodation in Canal Bank. Major G. F. EBERLE. on return to Division from Senior Officers Course at ALDERSHOT joined Company as Officer Commanding.	
	2&3		2 sections on CALIFORNIA shelters. 1 section preparing site for Camp for Pioneers at FRASCATY & section preparing Bn. H.Q. at HUBNER (D1C4.6) & shelters preparing Bn. H.Q. at ARRAS (D7A7.5) with so Inf. CLUSTER HOUSES. (D7B6.8). Bn OP dug at ARRAS. - Bn HQ CLUSTER houses repaired	
	4		2 sections working on shelters in CALIFORNIA. Reparation of ½ Zabern Coy instructions in cleaning & damming old German concrete shelters near ST JULIEN reinnumerated. Water Point near ST JULIEN. Reparation of ½ Zabern Coy instruction in cleaning & damming old German concrete shelters near MOUSE TRAP Farm. Sandbag walls round horses in H 36 & started as protection against bombs. Dim iron hut erected on West of CANAL. Work carried on Shelters in CALIFORNIA. St Julien Water Point	
	5		on above. St Julien Road Church of obstructions at ST JULIEN.	
	6,7,8		Moved to BROWNE Camp on POPERINGHE – ELVERDINGHE Rd Off Sior Workshops.	
	10		Rested Kit inspections etc.	
	11,12		Entrained at PESCHOEK at night. E. detraining train to started at 8.30 pm actually started at 12.15 am	
	13.			

A5834 Wt. W4973/M687 750,000 8/16 D. D. & L. Ltd. Forms/C.2118/13.

Army Form C. 2118.

WAR DIARY
or
INTELLIGENCE SUMMARY
(Erase heading not required.)

Instructions regarding War Diaries and Intelligence Summaries are contained in F.S. Regs., Part II. and the Staff Manual respectively. Title pages will be prepared in manuscript.

474TH (SOUTH MIDLAND) FIELD COMPANY, R.E.

Hour, Date, Place	Summary of Events and Information	Remarks and references to Appendices
October 14th 1917	Detrained at MAROEIL at 3:0 pm & marched to A.C.Q.	
15.	Coy in billets. Major Elwell & Capt. Roberts reconnoitred new area under guidance of 4th Canadian Field Coy.	
16	Took over from 4th Canadian Field Coy. 3 sections (minus) in dugouts at T.28 C.24. H.Q. 1 section at La TARGETE Sheet 36c.S.W.	
17	A.2.C.2.8 (Sheet 57B.N.W.) New area reconnoitred. Work carried on dugouts for Advanced Dressing Station in TED.O.G. GERRARD Sub.Coy H.Q. in QUEBEC. (T.17.C.59) 28th Div. took over line from 2nd Canadian Div.	
18	200 Inf. working party clearing back from 5' in T.O.&T. C.T. Length centuried. Sewers in VIMY-FARBUS ROAD between MERSEY C.T. & Grand Trunk R. C.T. continued	
19	As for 18th and R.E. Dump formed at CANADA where tramline cuts CANADA Trench. Rear Section on Camp Paths Roads and on old pits for Reger Poels. (143 Bde.)	
20	As 19th and a party of 20 Inf. repairing VANCOUVER Rd.	Lt. E.M Browne went in team 11th Ivry took charge of No 4 Section
21	As above	
22	As above & Tram line repaired between CANADA & QUEBEC	

1247 W 3299 200,000 (E) 8/14 J.B.C. & A. Forms/C. 2118/11.

Army Form C. 2118.

WAR DIARY
or
INTELLIGENCE SUMMARY
(Erase heading not required.)

474TH (SOUTH MIDLAND) FIELD COMPANY, R.E.

Instructions regarding War Diaries and Intelligence Summaries are contained in F. S. Regs., Part II. and the Staff Manual respectively. Title pages will be prepared in manuscript.

Hour, Date, Place	Summary of Events and Information	Remarks and references to Appendices
October 23rd 1917	as above	
24th	as above	Not action relieved No 2 Section infantry
25	area as for 24.15	Slight transfers from CANADA to ?
	Work as for 24.15	D.O.F.R. & C. prepared for mule Haulage
26	as above	12" Avenue Trench boarded.
27	as above	
28	as above	117th CJ Cooper 45 N.C.O received 21st Army mining school for some in support Canadians
29	as above	
30	as above	Excavation for Mess hut for Right Group H.Q. R.F.A started
31	as above	Major G.F.E. Bate hospital attacked Lt. 5.15 R Pumsor Primar to act as 2nd in Command.

O.C. 474th (S.M.) FIELD COY. R.E. (T).

/15 R Sussex

C.29

Vol 29

WAR DIARY or INTELLIGENCE SUMMARY

Army Form C. 2118

(Erase heading not required.)

Place	Date	Hour	Summary of Events and Information	Remarks and references to Appendices
M. CANAL BANK (N. of) YPRES	1.10.17 4.10.17		Work continued on front sector & tracks. "C" Coy moved up to CANAL BANK & worked on forward T.B. tracks	BELGIUM-FRANCE 22 N.W.
SIEGE CAMP (A.20.d.9)	12.10.17		Battalion moved from baking van from 20 KRRC (Relieving of 31st Divn helping attacks by 5th Army)	
"	13.10.17 14.10.17		A.O.R Killed 18 OR wounded 27 horses killed & wounded by one shell in Camp. Battn entrained at PESELHOEK for 1st Army area to join I Corps, & detrained at MAROEIL & marched here.	LENS
A.O.R.	15.10.17 16.10.17		Reconnoitred work of 2nd Canadian Pioneers.	
"			Battn. H.Q. & would have billets A & B Coys & transport in B.6.C. & front N. of NEUVILLE ST VAAST & C Coy Coy in B.5. N. of LES TILLEULS corner (most of THELUS) A Coy moved up to day work at ... B.6.9.	
BERTONVAL FARM	17.10.17		B Coy returned to A Coy.	
"	19.10.17		Work done in B.6. Coms mostly to PEGGY Trench flying & cleaning Trench B'. & track up to RAT TRAIL - on platoon making ... from Amphitheatre 6' in Coys in ... obtaining ... & repairing old road to BERTHONVAL FARM & ... Rifle Gp.	
"	23.10.17		Leaves in YPRES were had 2 Offr & 30 OR killed - 7 Offrs 226 OR wounded had 7 Offrs a number of O.R.s wounded remaining on duty.	

2/10/17

Rud Langham
Lt Col.
Cmd'g 1/5th R. Sussex Regt.
(Pioneers)

www.ingramcontent.com/pod-product-compliance
Lightning Source LLC
Chambersburg PA
CBHW081547160426
43191CB00011B/1863